5-91
9.00
Hotho
VER

D0860386

26,168

LC   Clark, Joe
5133
.P38 Laying down the law
C57
1989

DATE DUE

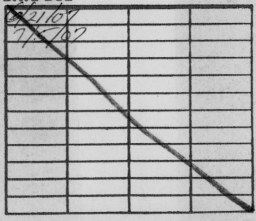

Laying down the law: Joe Clark's strateg
LC5133.P38C57 19   26168

Clark, Joe
   VRJC/WRIGHT LIBRARY

DEMCO

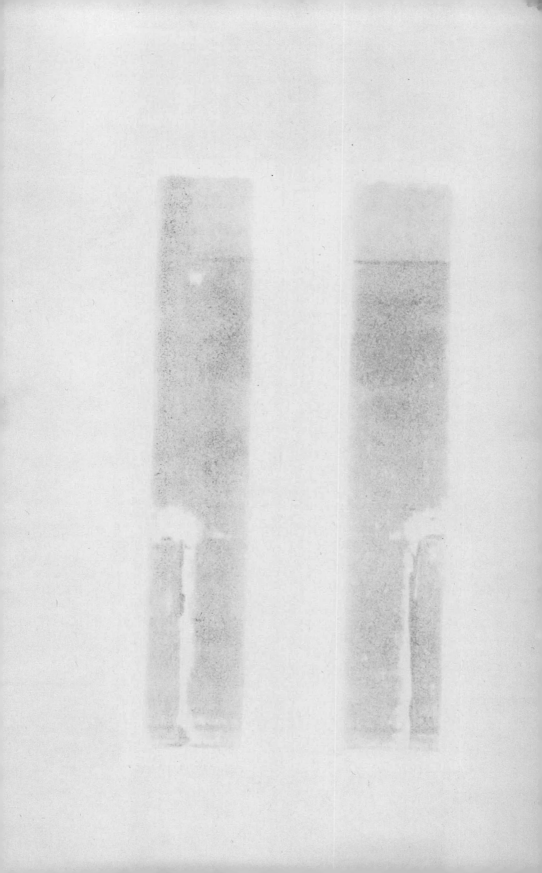

LAYING DOWN THE LAW

JOE CLARK'S STRATEGY FOR SAVING OUR SCHOOLS

LAYING DOWN THE LAW

JOE CLARK'S STRATEGY FOR SAVING OUR SCHOOLS

•

JOE CLARK
with
JOE PICARD

Assisted by Vincent A. Fusco

REGNERY GATEWAY

WASHINGTON, D.C.

VERNON REGIONAL
JUNIOR COLLEGE LIBRARY

Copyright © 1989 by Sound America, Inc.

All rights reserved. No part of this publication may be reproduced or transmitted in
any form or by any means, electronic or mechanical, including photocopy, recording,
or any information storage and retrieval system now known or to be invented, without
permission in writing from the publisher, except by a reviewer who wishes to quote
brief passages in connection with a review written for inclusion in a magazine,
newspaper or broadcast.

Library of Congress Cataloging-in-Publication Data

Clark, Joe, 1939 May 7–
Laying down the law : Joe Clark's strategy for saving our schools / Joe Clark with
Joe Picard.
p.   cm.
Includes index.
ISBN 0-89526-763-2 : $17.95
1. Education, Urban—New Jersey—Paterson—Case studies.
2. Eastside High School (Paterson, N.J.)   3. Clark, Joe, 1939 May 7–
I. Picard, Joe.   II. Title.
LC5133.P38C57   1989
373.749'23—dc20   89-31496
                                                                                                    CIP

Published in the United States by
Regnery Gateway
1130 17th Street, NW
Washington, DC 20036

and Reardon and Walsh
(a division of Summit Press Syndicate)
4028 N. Richland
Milwaukee, WI 53211

Distributed to the trade by
Kampmann & Company, Inc.
226 W. 26th Street
New York, NY 10001

Manufactured in the United States of America

10   9   8   7   6   5   4   3   2   1

ACKNOWLEDGMENTS

I DEDICATE this book to my loving wife, Hazel, and my three dear children, Joetta, Joe Jr., and Hazel, for their unswerving loyalty, and their ability to endure the tumult that my work in education has brought upon us.

I would also like to extend gracious thanks to the Reverend Frederick LaGarde, Superintendent of Schools Dr. Frank Napier, Mayor of Paterson Frank X. Graves, Kathryn McCabe, Veronica Maus, Jeanette Lyde, Florence Lopas, Henry Baker, Frank Colvin, Marilyn DiMartino, Frank Corrado, Arthur Larro, and Nini Judkins.

CONTENTS

viii · *Contents*

LAYING DOWN THE LAW

JOE CLARK'S STRATEGY FOR SAVING OUR SCHOOLS

1

THE ROAD TO DOOM

MOST PEOPLE generally know that inner-city schools in the United States are in bad shape, but they don't know how bad. These schools are *constant* Bedlam. There are fights every day. There is widespread incompetence, wanton destruction of property, and constant vile language. Prostitution is rampant. Violence is extolled. Weapons are prized, and used. Drugs are king. The major role model for the inner-city youth is the rich drug dealer. The main point of drug distribution is the school.

From New York and Chicago, from Washington, D.C., from Portland, from Houston, come stories of kids getting killed by other kids in gun battles over drug-dealing territory. In Detroit the shooting of children has averaged one per day. The principal cause of death among black teenage males is murder, usually by another black teenage male.

We are already paying for this deplorable mess. We are paying for jails and prisons. We are paying for increased police patrols. We are paying for increased emergency medical services for crime victims. We are paying for the rehabilitation of addicts. We are paying, through increases in prices, for the higher insurance rates businesses in or near the inner city must pay. We are paying for the teachers and administrators who do not do their jobs. And we can expect to be paying more and more for all of these things.

And that is but the iceberg's tip. There are one million school dropouts every year. Fifty percent of inner-city students, mostly blacks and Hispanics, drop out. There was a time in this country when a dropout could find a good enough blue collar job to survive, raise a family, and secure a modest yet decent piece of the American dream. Those days are gone.

We pay for unemployment. We pay for welfare. And the un-skilled dropout who can't get a job often turns to crime and drugs. The lowest estimated cost for these million dropouts per year is $60 billion. When lost tax revenues and losses from vandalism are factored in, the pricetag soars to an estimated $228 billion. Even at the lower estimate we are paying $60,000 per year per dropout. A year's worth of education per student costs between $3,000 and $4,000.

Of course we should try to keep the kids in school. But just doing that is scarcely enough, because the schools themselves, especially the inner-city schools, *don't teach them anything*. Grammar schools promote kids who have not learned the basics because of incompetent and cynical bureaucrats, administrators, and teachers who just don't want to be bothered and be-cause of a twisted sort of mind-set that doesn't want to bring disgrace upon minorities by admitting that large numbers of poor, minority kids aren't learning the three R's as quickly as their white and more affluent counterparts. The result is that large numbers of kids enter high school with third and fourth grade reading levels. The same mind-set and the same cynicism is functioning in the high schools. Education hardly goes on. Kids are pushed along through dumbed-down courses, to re-ceive diplomas that many of them cannot read. How are they supposed to hold down a job? Many inner-city youths with such worthless diplomas end up on the street.

There are at present between 30 million and 40 million func-tional illiterates in the United States. They cost the businesses of the nation an estimated $25 billion a year.

In October of 1988, the State of New York published a study on public education, the major finding of which was that there are, in actuality, two school systems, one for the affluent and one for the poor. The schools for the poor, the report said, "communicate low expectations and aspirations for their students, who are not given a full opportunity to succeed."

"Our society's acceptance of two unequal educational systems," the report continues, "is putting us at risk of creating a permanent underclass in New York and the nation. The existence of this underclass will ultimately erode the foundations of our democratic society."

This dire prophecy holds true not only for New York, but for the entire country. We are, at huge and steadily mounting costs to ourselves, creating a vast and permanent underclass that is shot through with drugs and violence, ignorance and resentment, frustration and anger, that will spill outwards into more affluent areas, bringing drugs, crime, and pitiable want. There are, at present, more homeless persons on America's streets than there have been at any time since the Great Depression. Seven hundred thousand of them are children.

How long can mainstream America turn its back on the crisis of the inner cities, like the foolish characters in Poe's *Masque of the Red Death* who fancied themselves safe from the raging plague? Will we wait until there's a bludgeoning robber behind each bush, until no garbage can goes unsearched for food scraps, until every fourth grader has tried crack? Will we let matters go until one of every two Americans cannot read, until the population is so uninformed and stupid that we vote to destroy the Constitution? Will we say it can't happen here until it does, until the drug gangs use suburban parks and shopping malls and neighborhoods for battlefields, until suburban youths join the skinheads in resurrecting Nazism, until there is an American version of the Final Solution, and no street is safe?

You can say that America's future is threatened by racial bigotry, or by the breakdown of the family, or by our national naivete toward world economic forces, or by a strange spiritual malady which has rendered us low-minded and irresponsible. And you would be right on each count—each is a contributing factor. But the major cause is ignorance. Again and again we do not see the main issues clearly enough or long enough. Again and again we do not discern which actions would truly be in our best interest. We take the wrong action, or settle for wrongheaded inaction. The cure for ignorance is education. But our schools, especially our inner-city schools, have broken down. This is a crisis in education.

Faith Popcorn is a marketing consultant for prestigious corporations. Each year she advises numerous Fortune 500 firms on what to expect—a sort of modern-day Sibyl, with an accuracy rating of 95 percent. She says, "We are falling so far behind in education that it is terrifying. I can see us becoming a fourth-rate power. All the mistakes of the past are being repeated. The children are not learning, they do not know their history."

They also do not know their math, their English, or their science. Yet these same corporations that Ms. Popcorn advises are in desperate need of trained, literate people. The jobs are there, jobs with pay sufficient to revive some American dreams, but the educational system, especially that of the inner cities where the training is most needed, is not there. The educational system is failing. We adults are failing our young people, leaving them unprepared, throwing them to the wolves, transforming them into the next ravenous pack.

Do not underestimate the danger. The world teaches the middle class and affluent youths to amass wealth by any means possible, and to hell with ethics and your fellow man. The world teaches the inner-city youth to amass wealth by the fastest, most evident means available—that usually means drugs and crime—and to hell with decency, family, and future. It is the responsibility of adults to start transmitting a different, higher message. The logical place to transmit the message is in the schools.

But will we? And before it's too late? Will inner-city adults stop tolerating incompetence and knavery in their children's educators? Will they shake from their television or drug daze and stop blaming everything on Whitey long enough to unite and demand leadership in their schools? Will the rest of America likewise stir, and wake up to the dire dimensions of the increasing crisis, and seek, find, and support genuine solutions? One thing is certain: Time is running out.

Schools are "the grand agent for the development or augmentation of national resources, more powerful in the production and gainful employment of the total wealth of a country than all the other things mentioned in the books of the political economists."

A great many things have changed since the renowned American educator, Horace Mann, wrote those words in the middle of the 19th century. Yet they are still absolutely true. It is up to us to work and make the promise of those words real again. It is up to us, all of us, to rescue our schools from the abyss.

My name is Joe Clark. For the last seven years I have been the principal of Eastside High School in Paterson, New Jersey, an inner-city school. In this book I will go into some detail on how I met the modern crisis in education at this particular school, and solved it there. I hope my story, and my advice, will help and inspire other individuals working to improve education. This is a task we must accomplish.

2

WELCOME TO EAST HELL

I WAS IN MY office at PS 6, on Carroll Street in Paterson, that May afternoon in May 1979, putting some papers in a briefcase, getting ready to head home. The secretary came in and handed me a weighty Manila envelope. "This was just messengered over from the superintendent's office," she said.

"Ah yes. The long-awaited report."

I had not requested a copy, but I knew I'd get one. That was Superintendent Napier's handwriting: *Attention Joe Clark.* I dropped it in my briefcase and walked out to my car.

On the ride home I thought about the event that had triggered this report—the Passaic County Prosecutor's report on Paterson's Eastside High School. The incident had happened on November 28 of the previous year.

A bunch of young hoodlums were heading for the school in the late morning. Maybe one or two were still so-called students, skipping classes as usual. The other three or four were dropouts, unemployed. All were stoned. I can picture them clearly. The tall, floppy hats, the long overcoats and bomber jackets, the phony and expensive gold chains. Strutting with shoulders back

8

and chests puffed out. Passing the joints. Arrogance and belligerence on their faces. Wildness and stupidity in their eyes.

Their talk was loud, crude, and boastful, and almost exclusively about weapons, drugs, and sex. Stuffed in their pockets were small bags of marijuana and smaller portions of cocaine wrapped in aluminum foil. There were also some switchblades. They were on their way to Eastside High, the busiest daytime black-market outlet in town.

They came up to the parking lot gate. Wide open, no one there to stop them. They knew exactly where to go. Hell, Eastside was their hangout as well as their place of business. Up to the side door of the south wing. No one there but a half dozen more so-called students, a couple whorey looking girls accompanying the "bad boys." They were lurking on the landing and just inside the door, smoking reefer, passing a pint. They had been waiting for the dope dealers. The little packages and the five and ten dollar bills started changing hands.

"See how easy, homeboy?" says one of the hoods to a wide-eyed novice, as he increases his roll by several bills.

Another youth opens the door. "Guard up top!" he warns.

"Who cares," snaps one of them, adding some expletives. "He's gonna stay up top." That is, he'll stay in the corridor, won't enter the stairwell area, and certainly won't come down to the door or outside.

"I'll slice him if he comes down!" boasts another, eliciting laughter, and further boasts and vulgarities.

The guard, predictably, passes by. He doesn't even glance through the inside glass door, though he knows people are out there. In fact, he doesn't look *because* he knows they're out there.

The deals and the dope-taking go on. The foolish girls get handled. When the lunch bell rings the hoodlums head inside. They go stealthily up the stairs to the hall door, because they know that the only person who would dare challenge their entry—Mr. Brown, the history teacher, whose classroom door abuts that corridor entrance—might be watching. But as loud, disorderly bunches of kids come traipsing and running along the corridor toward the cafeteria, one by one the dope-dealing hoodlums slip in unseen and tramp along with the rest.

I know this is what they did. It's what they always did.

The cafeteria. Easily mistaken for Milton's Pandemonium. Radios blasting, kids screaming, food flying, fights forever breaking out. Dope being sold every day. During the regime at Eastside B.C. (Before Clark), teachers utterly, and understandably, detested drawing cafeteria duty. During classes a teacher could at least lock the door and deal with a relatively small chunk of potential or actual chaos. In the cafeteria all the dikes were down. Teacher-monitors were helpless and concerned mainly for their own safety. The kids, of course, readily perceived this. Bedlam reigned.

On this day a quiet, amiable math teacher, James Piombino, was one of the unlucky ones to draw cafeteria duty. He was a good math teacher, and a man of real integrity, but just as impotent in those wild precincts as any solitary human being, short of an armed Marine, would be.

He was stationed just outside the cafeteria, in a fairly isolated place where students and interlopers often milled about, coming from and returning to the cafeteria. This traffic in and out the exit, as well as the loitering, were against school regulations, but the math teacher was a realist; he knew it was senseless to try to enforce these rules when he would get little if any support from the guards (wherever they might be) and none at all from the principal's office. Every few minutes he would, with scant results, remind the kids to be quiet and to move along. He waited impatiently for his duty to end.

But he saw something he could not honorably ignore. A girl walked past a pair of boys, and one of the boys made a loud and vulgar pass at her. She snapped something in reply. The male youth, one of the non-student hoodlums who had snuck into the cafeteria, probably to sell dope, hurled several insults at the girl, then raced up, grabbed her, swung her around, and punched her.

Piombino, tall and thin, pushed through the onlooking students, and wrapped the shorter, violent youth in a bear hug. The miscreant wriggled and kicked, and yelled for his buddies. Suddenly the math teacher, who was trying to haul the youth to a corridor where he might get some help, was jumped by two more young males. One leaped on his back, punching him, while the other tackled him at the knees. The first youth broke free as Piombino fell to the floor, and all three thugs punched and kicked the teacher. He scrambled to his feet, arm raised to protect his head, and noticed, as the assault continued, that 20 or more students were watching, not offering help, just watching.

At least one student, however, had gone for help. The three hoods, cursing Piombino, decided to bolt. They raced by the guard coming to the teacher's assistance. They ran down the corridor, whooping and hollering, and left the building without any resistance. They were never identified.

The math teacher escaped serious injury, and the girl was unhurt. But Piombino and the rest of the teaching staff were in a state of terror. Small wonder. Though Eastside had been an abomination among high schools throughout the 1970s—with dope rings, sex rings, vandalism, and violence—since the start of the 1978 school year, the hellishness had been escalating at an alarming rate. The attack on Mr. Piombino was only the most recent in a rash of assaults. One teacher had been flung up against a blackboard. Another had been slapped and spat upon. Yet another had been kicked several times. A security guard had been mugged. Several teachers and guards had had knives drawn on them and their lives threatened. One teacher had a pistol waved under his nose. Another teacher was so terrified that, when a wise guy pointed a banana at him, he thought he was going to be shot.

People chuckle about that now. Few did then. Most teachers felt that it was only a matter of time before someone would be critically injured, even killed. Piombino had been defenseless, utterly vulnerable. If one of the thugs had used a switchblade. . . .

This is to say nothing of the daily barrage of verbal abuse teachers received, the constant havoc in the corridors, and the repeated acts of vandalism upon the automobiles of teachers and administrative staff. Teach under such circumstances? You might as well try reading Hamlet to a hurricane.

The next day a reporter from *The Paterson Evening News* went to the school. The administration, true to its wishy-washy nature, tried to downplay the story, as if a violent attack upon an instructor in a school building was no cause for concern. Typical. But numerous teachers, as fed up with their do-nothing principal as they were frightened of the hoodlums who terrorized the school, ran off a litany of incidents to the reporter.

The News' headline for the following evening, November 30, declared: FEAR STALKS CITY HIGH SCHOOL.

On December 1, the Passaic County Prosecutor's Office met with the Paterson chief of police, the superintendent of schools, members of the Board of Education and other high-ranking officials, to discuss the situation at Eastside High. They appointed a committee and inaugurated an investigation. Their findings and recommendations were in the 40-page report in my briefcase.

Stepping inside the front door of my home, I met and embraced each member of my family: my two teenage children, Joetta and Joe, my wife Hazel, and our darling infant Hazel. I held each a little closer, a little longer, thinking. Then, just before dinner, I tackled the manuscript.

"Paterson Eastside High School: A Microcosm of the Conflict, Turmoil and Violence in U.S. Schools."

That was on the cover. Within I found much that was sadly true:

- "the present security system is woefully inadequate and inefficient"
- "Committee members ... were never asked for identification or questioned as to their reasons for being in the school"
- "various entrances to the school were completely unwatched"
- "guards ... complained that the administration did not support them in punishing students brought to the office"
- "teachers complained that their efforts to discipline a student are not fully supported by the administration"
- "a chain of command is virtually non-existent"
- "Drugs are brought into the school not only by individual students and non-students, but also by gangs who both use and sell"
- "readily detected the smell of marijuana"
- "all too common incidents of vandalism, extortion and larceny"
- "Assaults of students and teachers take place for a variety of reasons which run the gamut from robbery to revenge to outright viciousness"
- "some students bring weapons into the school"
- "Doors and locks are broken. Window breakage is prevalent. Graffiti is evident."
- "overcrowding, tardiness and truancy"
- "Eastside served as a 'dumping ground' for teachers who did not, or could not, function adequately in other Paterson schools"

- "lack of communication between parents and the school"
- "benefit a school can bestow on a student is severely limited without parent interest, support, cooperation."

I put down the report and closed my eyes. Though I well knew Eastside's ignominious condition without the aid of an official report, reading those pages through had fired my indignation once again. What a disgrace! They ought to demote that whole administration to plucking up litter in the parking lot.

After dinner I stationed myself by the telephone and, in about ten minutes, it rang. No clairvoyance was involved. It would have been a wonder if this call had not come.

"Evening, Joe," said the superintendent. "Read the report?"

"Good evening to you, Frank. Of course I have. It's well-written. It's accurate. Only it doesn't tell plainly and fully enough the deficiency of the administration. Sometimes you've got to call a wimp a wimp."

"It's angered you. Good. I love a man who gets fired up for the right reasons. Joe, I want you to take over at Eastside. You're the only one who could make a real difference."

I'd known for some time that this was coming. Frank Napier had been awaiting the prosecutor's report so he could present Joe Clark to the Board of Education, saying something to the effect of "drastic predicaments call for drastic measures," because Joe Clark, despite the "Miracle on Carroll Street"—the name parents gave the sweeping reforms and massive improvement I engineered at PS 6, which had been (B.C.) the grammar school equivalent of Eastside—was still too outspoken and too radical for many officials in the Paterson school system. Not for Frank Napier, however, who agreed with my philosophy and knew that I could put it in action.

"I'll be beside you all the way," he said, when I made no immediate reply. "I'll give you all the support you'll need. Together we can make something happen at that snakepit."

I love a challenge. Especially one that will exercise the scope and strength of my abilities. Nonetheless, I turned down Superintendent Napier's offer.

"Why?"

"It's my responsibility to my own kids. They need their father here, at least my two teenagers do, until they graduate from high school. With PS 6 I can just manage and not feel I am slighting either the school children or my own. But Eastside. Eastside is a monster, Frank. It's a mythological hydra if there ever was one. It would take up all my time to do the job right. I cannot give it all my time just now, and I won't take a job I cannot do right."

He tried talking me into it. We traded reasons for a few minutes. Finally I said, "You've got administrative hypocrites there now. Do you want another?"

"What do you mean?"

"Frank, how am I going to teach those kids to be responsible adults or convince their parents to be responsible mothers and fathers while I'm shirking my own parental responsibility? It just won't wash."

"All right, all right. But what's going to happen now?"

What happened was more of the same. For the next three years. You could have a bible full of sound recommendations, (and many of those of the prosecutor's report were quite good), but lacking individuals with the desire and managerial skill to understand and implement them, they are not much more than paper and ink. The improvement, for example, of the relationships between teacher and student, parent and school, administrator and teacher, requires philosophical insight and dedicated, persistent, hands-on work. And this spirit of genuine work must originate from the principal's office—which at Eastside it emphatically did not. The only improvement from the time of the report (May 1979) until the time of my appointment (May 1982) was an increase in the number of security guards from 13 to 18. The hoodlums easily learned how to avoid (or deal drugs to) the five extra guards. The only result of this "improvement" was to increase the cost of the payroll.

Eastside High remained a virulent microcosm of all the malignant forces in present-day American schools.

For example. In the Fall of 1981, a female Hispanic student went to her favorite teacher with a problem. The student's mother and older brother were periodically beating her. It seems these two ghetto-dwellers were members of a cult, some horrid contortion of the Christian faith, which believed that the devil inhabited the bodies of certain people and had to be physically beaten out. So, in the name of God and love, they were brutally thrashing this 18-year-old.

The teacher was appalled. She went to the principal. He wasn't available. The next day she hunted him down, finally buttonholed him, and told him the story.

"I think," he reportedly said, "you should leave this one alone. It's a domestic affair, and the girl is no longer a minor. Besides, she's probably exaggerating."

"I don't think she is. She showed me some bruises on her arms."

But Eastside's chief administrator was content to attribute these bruises to the wildness of the girl, a girl he did not know, and reiterated that the teacher ought not pursue the matter any further.

The teacher saw the girl again, to assure herself that there had been no mendacity or exaggeration. She came away convinced that the 18-year-old was receiving severe and frequent beatings, as well as having disgusting degradations and crazed proselytism heaped upon her daily. The teacher returned to the principal.

"Sir, I am positive that she is getting beaten by her mother and her brother."

The principal, according to the young teacher, replied, "I specifically told you to leave this matter alone. We are not the girl's parents."

"Parents!" the teacher exclaimed. "She is terrified of going home. She has nowhere to turn but us. She came to me seeking help. I can't turn my back on her."

"You can and you will!" he reportedly thundered. "You will follow my instructions and let this matter drop or I will personally see to it that you do not make tenure. Am I quite clear?"

The teacher was still a year away from tenure, and she knew the principal was capable of making good his threat to wreck her career. Distraught, she went to the Education Association representative. This woman, a veteran teacher at Eastside, was outraged. She was also smart enough to know that there was no dealing with this sorry excuse for an administrator from a subordinate position. Fortunately, there was an alternative.

Superintendent Napier, indignant over repeated reports that

Eastside was as bad, if not worse, under this principal, as it had been under his unsuccessful predecessor, had for a time put himself in residence in an office in the school's basement. He was there at the time of this incident, and the teachers' representative, knowing the kind of man the superintendent is, did not hesitate to go to him. She related the whole story as they walked from one office to another.

Frank Napier halted his steps and boomed, "He said what?" His voice reverberated along the corridor. "I will pay that so-called administrator a visit at once. No teacher in any school I am superintendent of is going to lose tenure for trying to help a student!"

"Oh no! No, no, no," was the principal's reply, "I would never deny a deserving teacher tenure. Never, sir. Never."

"And what about the abused student?"

"Well, I'd like to help of course. But you see, we don't have the proper facilities here to deal with such problems."

"What about the school psychiatrist?"

"Eastside doesn't have one."

Napier's muscles tensed, his brow darkened, his eyes blazed. "What do you mean Eastside does not have a psychiatrist! I know the school psychiatrist. I had coffee with him three days ago!" I wonder how my predecessor must have felt at that moment, a chief administrator who had not even acquainted himself with the offices under his command. "Come with me," ordered the superintendent, who led him to the psychiatrist's office, two corridors and a staircase away.

The psychiatrist saw the troubled student. After one meeting he recommended that the matter be brought at once to the civil authorities. The outcome was that the girl was removed from the custody of her mother and sent by jet to the home of her grandparents in Panama.

What would have happened, I wonder, if Dr. Napier had not been in residence at the school?

If the superintendent still harbored any doubts about the crying need for a complete administrative overhaul to rescue education at Eastside, he was thoroughly disabused of them several weeks later in that same school year.

While walking along the corridor he smelled something. Marijuana. He followed the unmistakable odor to a stairwell and surprised two males. One bolted, but Napier had the other one cornered. The punk pulled out a switchblade. "Back off, you old fool!" he shouted, as he popped the blade and waved it under the superintendent's chin. "Let me by or I'll cut you bad!"

I know Frank Napier. He is built like a bull and has the courage of a lion. There was no hesitation. His hand lashed out and seized the punk's wrist in a strong grip, forcing to one side the blade's threat, while his other hand grasped the miscreant by the shirt. The hood, in surprise and terror, dropped the knife and Frank proceeded to, in his own words, "kick his ass."

It was afterwards that he seriously considered closing the school entirely. There was no order, no education was taking place, and, while he was through with this principal, there were no other aspiring candidates for the post. That job, principal of Eastside High, had, 20 years ago, been the plum of the education jobs in Paterson. Now it was anathema.

Then he remembered me. "Both your older kids will have graduated from high school by this June," he said. "So don't hand me any excuses. I want you to be principal at Eastside."

"Only if you and the board will let me do my job."

"You have my complete support. Deliver, and you'll have the board's as well."

I knew Eastside, knew the great energy and constancy the task would require. I was well aware what the words meant when I said "I accept." As I've mentioned, I love a challenge. I love education, too.

In May 1982, when my appointment had not yet been officially announced but was being bruited about, I paid a number of informal visits to Eastside, looked around, and talked to some teachers.

"Welcome to East Hell, Mr. Clark," said one gym teacher.

An English teacher, attempting to keep things humorous, added, "What does that portal sign in Dante say? 'Abandon every hope, ye that enter.' "

"No offense to the great poet," I said. "But I'm having that sign removed."

They were polite and incredulous, and I, not wanting to discuss my plans, changed the subject and soon moved away. But that grim quotation stuck with me. Hope abandoned. It was worse than the "dream deferred" of Langston Hughes, and more accurate in describing the prevalent present-day attitude toward inner-city education. I watched the students exiting the building, and the grave words echoed in my mind. The system abandons them and, far worse, they abandon their dreams, their real opportunities. I cannot, I thought, change the economy or age-old prejudice or the system at large. But what I can, must, and will stop is the way these young people destroy themselves. I will return them their hope. I pledged myself to showing them how to fulfill their better dreams.

Insight A
A Day in the Life of a School
•

Shortly after learning I would be at Eastside, I imagined myself in the shoes of the students, the decent youths, whose lives I intended to snatch back from the abyss. I would mentally follow this one and that one through their daily paces. I grew up in one ghetto, spent much of my professional career in another, and triumphed over both. From bottom to top I know our urban wasteland and the people, good and bad, who inhabit it. The little slice of life story I'm about to tell, though imaginary, definitely reflects reality.

An alarm goes off next to William's bed. Time to get up and get ready for school. The prospect depresses him. He thinks of his grandmother, a good hard-working woman who, before she died, impressed upon him the need for education. She said, "A good education is the only way you're going to get out of this ghetto." William valued her advice. He wanted an education. That's why the thought of going to school depressed him. Seventeen-year-old William was smart enough to know he wasn't getting one there.

But, he has reckoned, there are no other options. If he quit school and spent each day at the Public Library educating himself, there would be no diploma, no chance of attending college or of finding a decent job. He sits at the edge of the bed, staring at the carpetless floor, and for a moment feels like crying. He takes a deep breath, resolves himself, and stands up.

The room is cold and there is no hot water this gray November morning. William makes do, gets dressed and goes into the kitchen. He lives with his mother, his four younger sisters, and an infant nephew, in the second floor apartment of a run-down house on Poplar Street, about a half-mile from Eastside High. It has been about a year since his older brother was shot dead in a gang fight over turf and drugs. Before that an older sister had driven off with some pimp. Both brother and sister had been Eastside dropouts. So had William's father, who has not been heard from for more than seven years.

William's 16-year-old sister, who is snoring away while

VERNON REGIONAL
JUNIOR COLLEGE LIBRARY

her unattended baby wails, was also an Eastside dropout. She is on welfare now and, though she hasn't told anyone yet, is pregnant again. She likes getting those monthly checks—the first steady income she's ever had, except for a few tempestuous weeks at McDonald's—and she now looks forward to more government money, to keep her in gin, marijuana, and cheap jewelry. William regularly reads her the more complicated mail from the welfare agency. Complicated mail to this 16-year-old mother means just about anything beyond "See Jane run." William's mother is only a bit more literate, and he performs similar duties for her. She is also on welfare, also without a job, but does at least try, now and again, to find work, though never with much success. Her illiteracy and her obvious drug addiction (supported by a boyfriend-pusher) have closed door after door in her dull-eyed and ravaged face.

She is sitting in the kitchen, staring out the window. The youngest daughter, age 4, is running around barefoot and is nearly as filthy as the smock she's been wearing for almost a week. William's 11-year-old sister struts into the kitchen in a skirt so high and tight that William, grimacing, says she looks like a whore. She fires back some words that are not allowed on network television. While William woofs down some cereal and smacks an occasional cockroach, his mother starts complaining about her nasty boyfriend, her runaway daughter, her daughter the mother, her 14-year-old who had attempted suicide after aborting a fetus, the government, the last two places to refuse her employment, Whitey in general, God, and, most of all, the man who had deserted her, William's father.

The father had certainly been irresponsible, and just as certainly an alcoholic. He was neither mean-spirited nor a drunk when they got married. Yes, he was a dropout, but in those days there were still some jobs for unskilled laborers who were willing to work hard. He had a factory job that paid good money and offered a lot of overtime. They had lived in a better apartment when William was a baby. They had talked about buying a house in a nicer section of town. But then, suddenly, the factory shut down. The company was a subsidiary of a large corporation, whose board of directors had concluded that it was more profitable to the shareholders to exploit the much cheaper labor market overseas. The job William's father had been doing is now being done by a Taiwanese man, at a wage less than one-third what the father had received. The dream of their own house vanished. William's father, without the aid of a diploma, took one degrading job after another. He also took to the bottle. And one day he just took off.

William's mother was too embittered and her mind too befuddled by drugs to view her husband's case in an economic or educational light. Yet it had been transmitted to her on the TV news. What had happened in Paterson that had cost her husband his factory job was not an isolated incident. Rather, it was a small segment of a large, continuing, and irreversible trend. American corporations are moving their manufacturing operations overseas, to Taiwan, South Korea, and elsewhere. This is the post-Industrial Age. Blue collar jobs are fast disappearing and the vast majority of these jobs are probably never coming back.

This painful truth strikes the urban areas with particular poignancy. At the same time, both the dropout rate and illiteracy are up, especially among urban minorities. Unfortunately, a large portion of the United States' population is receiving a poorer education at the very point in history when America needs technological and informational intelligence, which means educated individuals, as never before.

William had heard somewhere about the dwindling job market for unskilled laborers. He had as well his grandmother's wise words and a goodly amount of horse sense, and knew his father's chances would have been better had the man possessed a high school education. The healthy mind takes advantage of the best opportunity available, no matter how limited and constricted it might at first appear. To give up is to lose. He kisses his mother, grabs his books, and heads out, intent on snatching back a chance in life.

He walks alone past rows of decrepit houses, abandoned factory buildings, drug-gang haunts, and empty lots full of trash and rubble. He pauses when he sees no one around, takes the two dollars his mother had given him for lunch and stuffs it down his sock, to protect it from gang members who might be extorting money. Pressure has been exerted upon him to join one or another of the gangs, especially the one his slain brother had been in. He has resisted, despite being beaten, labelled a coward, and having his life threatened. The fate of his brother and the dull gaze from his mother's eyes had steeled William against the use of drugs, though they are everywhere and all gang members offer "free highs" to prospective newcomers. And there was also the get-rich-quick temptation.

William has seen it happen to kids he knew. A gang member offers a youngster so many vials of crack to sell to other youths—the most convenient daytime marketplace for such poison being, of course, the school. The first time, the young dupe can keep all the money he makes. The second time, he has to return a certain percentage to his supplier. Yet he is still seeing money like never before, and for almost no work at all, unloading an escapist and addictive drug to eager morons within the halls of an institution where the authorities had abdicated all responsibility.

One after another these novice drug-dealers, these prospective cons and corpses, leap into the snakepit of that money-sweetened fool's paradise. They called themselves "bad," thought they were big men. Bad indeed. In reality they are the imbecilic puppets of criminal drug lords whose business means the destruction of their brothers and sisters. Soon they are hooked on what they peddle; so much for their profits. They are also inextricably caught up in the criminal gang, and follow its sick blood-code as though it were a law of nature; so much for their freedom. So much for their future.

These big men. Probably no one (at home, on the street, or in the classroom) had ever told them what constitutes a real man. Often I wonder how many deluded youths have been lost because of adults who have failed to set examples of real manhood and real womanhood.

As William approaches the school building, he sees where the chain-link fence has been ripped apart, so that the drug-thugs and pimps can carry on their skulduggery on the school grounds during the night as well. He notices that the hole has gotten larger. The yard is filled with the chaotic sound of twenty different ghetto-blasters, and already there are whiffs of marijuana in the air. He sees boys he knows are not students, as well as certain felonious figures that could no longer be called boys. He sees a younger student getting bullied for money. A bevy of heavily made-up girls are yattering about their sexual encounters.

The bell rings. William enters the school, resigned to the hollering mob that shoves through the door and runs along the corridors, spitting, cursing, and brawling. The walls are covered with graffiti. William spies a drug deal going on at one of the entrances, a security guard taking part in the transaction.

William enters a classroom. It is pandemonium. Students are shouting and laughing. They stand on their desks, they run around, they throw things. The teacher glares at them. They revile him, and he reviles them back. He calls them "social refuse" and "unteachable barbarians." Then he sits at his desk and reads the newspaper, declaring that he can do nothing until order is restored, though he raises not a pinky to restore it, and only occasionally looks up to trade curse for curse.

This is supposed to be a math class and William knows he needs help. Finally he takes his textbook (one of the few in the room) and goes up to the sullen teacher. In response to his question, William is told that the teacher cannot be expected to teach anything in these hellish conditions, and that the teacher is not a teacher anymore but a zookeeper. But William persists, and the cynic behind the desk at last responds with a quick and cold explanation of method and solution. There is virtually no communion, no joy of teaching, no joy of learning. William knows he must settle for this. He must also endure mockery from classmates.

Other classes are not much different: always the same wild disorder, with fluctuations in the degree and decibel-level of the chaos; fights periodically breaking out, threats hurled at teachers and other students; pencils, erasers, and pennies thrown at teachers. An English instructor receives a vicious kidney punch in the hall, yet refuses to divulge the name of the assailant for fear of reprisal. The drug market does steady business all day long. The weapons market also is active. Illicit sexual activity is conducted brazenly. A few teachers actually try practicing their profession: opening books, writing on the board, trying to shout the lesson above the chaos. In vain. A history teacher manages to oversee a brief quiz. Some results: The French Revolution took place in the 1960s, Napoleon was the tank general for Hitler, James Madison invented ice cream, the Rosetta Stone was a rare pink gem worn by a sultan, a Tory is a kind of fish.

It was that alleged inventor of ice cream, James Madison, who wrote: "A popular government without popular information or the means of acquiring it, is but a prologue to a farce or a tragedy, or perhaps both."

Young William, at one point in that deranged morning, puts his hands to his head and mutters, "Is this ever going to change?"

We all might ask ourselves the same question. Can the monstrous patterns ever be changed? What can be done about the young who see no value in education and consequently learn nothing, who attack and denigrate authority, consort with criminals, take drugs, get pregnant, go on welfare, drop out, remain unemployed, and sink deeper into drugs and crime. Their children are raised in illiterate, anti-educational homes. Then they attend anti-educational schools that are infected with cynical teachers who do not teach, and are run by cowardly administrators who do not prevent violence and chaos from overwhelming all. The grim cycle repeats. And what, in the meantime, happens to all those decent-hearted kids, like William, who want to learn? Must they abandon every hope?

No!

It *will* change, William my son. It *must*. I do not know when for Chicago or Jersey City or Los Angeles. But for Eastside High in Paterson, New Jersey, it has changed. Because I accepted the challenge. I went to Eastside and created a High School.

Let me tell you how.

3

THE FACELIFT

WILLIAM J. BENNETT, the newly appointed Secretary of Education, did not wait for us to finish lunch. Indeed, it had just been served, when he started firing questions at me.

"What was the biggest problem you faced when you took over at Eastside?"

"Hoodlums."

"What is it now?"

"Bureaucrats."

He did not ask for elaboration, but went rapidly on to the next shot, with two or three of his aides taking notes, giving me but a few brief intervals to appreciate the delicious food.

"Have the MBS [Minimum Basic Skills] scores gone up?"

"Every year."

"Satisfied?"

"No. They could be higher."

It was early March 1986. The day outside the tall windows of the secretary's dining hall was gray and wintry. There were about 12 of us seated at the long table in that elegant, high-ceilinged room: the secretary, members of his staff, four Eastside teachers, and myself. We were there, of course, at his invitation. He knew that in the last few years I had been the guest of several members of the administration, including the President himself and Bennett's predecessor at Education, Terrel Bell. He also knew that I had spoken to a Senate subcommittee on the state of education in the United States. But he was intent on questioning me himself. I had been brought to Washington neither for a diplomatic pat-on-the-back photo opportunity nor for any other politically motivated formality. I was there to be interrogated and scrutinized. Bill Bennett wanted to see for himself if Joe Clark was the McCoy.

I must say I liked and appreciated this: a man stepping into a managerial position who, from the start, really was the boss, his focus not on the perquisites of his position, but on the necessary work to be done and the "how" of doing it. He reminded me of myself.

So I took no umbrage at his brusque inquisition, saying to myself, "It's his style." However, when the secretary threw a certain series of questions my way, I welcomed them with hidden yet playful and good-hearted delight. Because I and everyone else there could see that my sphinx-faced replies had begun to perplex, and even annoy, Mr. Bennett.

"How long," he asked, "did it take you to establish order at Eastside?"

"One day."

An eyebrow went up. No rapid following question this time. Rather a pause, filled with the sound of aides shifting in their seats and silver clinking china. The secretary fixed me, and I could feel the others' eyes upon me. But, having been permitted no explanations before, I was not going to volunteer information now.

Secretary Bennett tried a little chicken, then fired again. "Well, how long was it before you got all those kids to walk to the right?"

I suppressed a smile. "One day."

"One day?"

"That's correct."

"And how long to run out the hoods and drug-dealers?"

"One day."

His brow darkened, his face was stern. He glanced at a pair of his aides, and the three exchanged incredulous looks. "A single day to establish order and to run the hoods out of what was formerly one of the most turbulent high schools in the nation. That's rather remarkable."

I said nothing. Let him ask me how.

"That one day, Principal Clark, that was your first day?"

"The first day, Mr. Secretary."

It was obvious that he did not believe me. "And the teachers. How long did it take for them to adjust to the new regulations?"

"Sir, one day."

"One day?" He was getting a little hot now, assuming I was blowing up my achievements to impress him. "All this in a single day? Mr. Clark, it seems to me that. . . ."

"Excuse me, Mr. Secretary." It was one of the Eastside teachers, who had taken it upon herself to interject. I was willing to go another round or two before clearing up the mystery, but I guess she just got a little nervous. "Principal Clark is not," she said, "being totally open with you."

"Oh no?" he said. "In what way?"

"The transformation he brought about at Eastside did, for the most part, take place in one day, the first day," she explained. "What he has not told you is that he was able to do this because he had been at the school six and seven days a week, eight and ten and twelve hours a day, all that summer long, carefully laying down his program's foundation, and getting all the necessary innovations and changes in place. Everything was ready. That's why the first day went like magic."

"Oh, I see," said the Secretary of Education. He leaned back in his chair and seemed to relax a little for the first time that meeting. The tension disappeared from his countenance, the incredulity from his voice. "I see it all now." He smiled at me. "You're a nuts and bolts man. You're into thorough management."

Precisely, Mr. Secretary.

I had visited Eastside a few times toward the end of the 1981–82 school year, before my appointment as principal became public. On my first such visit, on the afternoon following my conversation with Dr. Napier, I spent some time standing unobtrusively in the parking lot, looking at the school building.

It is a massive, tan brick, three-story building, constructed in a conservative version of the "college Gothic" style, with a smaller, modern, white concrete annex to one side. It has 115 rooms, 26 sets of doors, and banks of large, rectangular windows across its broad front. It looks, in many ways, like a lot of the older, still structurally sound school buildings around the nation. I recall reflecting on the architecture: how this style had so often been chosen for its emblematic value, signifying the sober, serious pursuit of higher levels of learning, with yet loftier, more promising peaks in the offing.

Even as I contemplated this my eye fell upon the crooked line of a cracked window. Following this down, I saw that the window below was also transected by an irregular line, and the one next to it was shattered, a spray of white in the corner where the rock had hit. There were other broken windows with jagged edges of glass still in the frames, which invited moronic hoods to snap off shards, threaten and, at times, rip people. And now my eye had descended to the front steps and ground level, where I observed the profuse, vulgar, and frenzied graffiti that belted the building.

I walked up closer, to read selections from this inner-city bible of madness. Classes had ended less than an hour before, and the place was nearly empty. Some janitors and guards were about, putting in their hours, as well as a few teachers and minor administrators. But that big school building, which should have radiated evidence of the noble ideals for which it stood, emanated desolation and was a reflection of the ghetto's desolate soul.

I knew that when darkness fell the parking lot would become an arena for demonic activity, and the building a target for abuse and burglary.

As high as the spray can could reach there were the weird codes of vainglorious gangs, grotesque and obscene depictions, imprecations and denigrations of students, teachers, and administrators, egotistical rantings, encomiums to drugs and violence, every profanity imaginable, and all sorts of idiotic declarations. For example: *Burn yor buks wit a blow torch!*

No, no, I said to myself as I walked away, it's the graffiti that's going, not the books.

One of the first things I did that summer was to confer with the head of maintenance for the Paterson school system and rent a capable sandblaster. The grinding and booming whir was a symphony to my ears. I often stepped outside in the bright day and watched the vile scribblings get blasted to oblivion. The sober strength of the old building began to shine through with the beauty of renewal.

"Looks great," I said, shouting over the noise to a workman.

"Yeah, sure," he replied. "But howya gonna keep it that way?"

"With another kind of sandblaster," I said. "A more powerful model."

He gave me a puzzled look. "Whattaya mean?"

I smiled. "I'm going to blast this whole school. I don't mean just the building, but the whole school and everyone in it, and everyone connected with it. Know what I mean?"

He was skeptical. "You got a blaster that good?"

I raised my index finger and tapped my head. "Right up here."

"Oh man!" he said. "Good luck!"

"Thanks. But luck has very little to do with it."

There was even more graffiti inside the building than there was outside. The walls were an atrocity of drivel in ink, graphite, lipstick, and paint. The restrooms, male and female, were a total abomination. This was clear testimony that chaos, once allowed to take command, knows no limits. It will encourage the most timid and introverted youngster to wax brazen and scribble some tidbit of perverse or anarchic garbage. It also represented the "mene, tekel, upharsim" for 25 years of incompetent administrators. It took no Daniel to decipher that surely their reigns were numbered and broken if they could not quash and control these outpourings.

"One of my first concerns," I told the superintendent over the phone, "is to give this building the appearance of respectability. I am well aware that appearance is nothing without substance. But if an institution has substance—which, I assure you, the new Eastside will have—especially when it is regaining substance for the first time in decades, then it is absurd to put forth a shoddy, run-down appearance. That would only be an invitation to disrespect and further abuse."

"Just tell me what you need, Joe," he replied.

"More paint and more painters."

"You're on. Bill what paint you need and I'll temporarily assign Eastside extra maintenance laborers. What else?"

I laughed. "Do you have a few hours?"

The restrooms needed extensive work. Toilet seats had been ripped out, mirrors and lights were broken, toilet stall doors hung by single hinges, drains were deliberately clogged. Throughout the building there were numerous instances of cracked and shattered glass. In the classrooms, blackboards had been split and many desks were damaged beyond repair. Clocks had been ruined and loudspeaker outlets punctured. Tables in the cafeteria had been wrecked. About half the entrance-exit doors could be opened from the outside. There were innumerable other miscellaneous defacings and breakages, and the marks of neglect. The entire school stank of mustiness, tobacco, marijuana, spilled alcohol and soda, and urine.

Then there was the damage caused by theft. Classrooms, offices, laboratories, the janitors' closets, the gym, the library—all had been burglarized at one time or another, and most more than once. Whatever appeared to possess resale value, and could be carried out, was. Other things were destroyed out of sheer spite. In the corridors, trophies were stolen from their display cases, copper piping was ripped out, fire extinguishers and axes were pilfered, as were the brass nozzles of the fire hoses. Sometimes they took the entire hose.

These thefts, although figures on the subject are impossible, most assuredly went to the procurement of drugs. It was one more level on which the school was being attacked by hell itself.

I made repeated, unannounced, personal inspections of the school. I looked in every classroom and office, each lab and each closet. I toured the basement, walked on the roof, visited the boiler room. I'm sure I sent shock waves through the janitorial staff, many of whom now faced the hard realization that they would be required to work for their paychecks. I read every report of vandalism at the school. I drew up my own list of thefts and breakages, and was not very surprised to discover that a large amount of damage had gone unreported, or was listed in reports that had been lost.

"Every broken object has got to be repaired or replaced," I said to Dr. Napier. "And the areas that don't need paint nonetheless need a washing."

"We'll go for it, the whole ball of wax," said the superintendent. "It is very much a matter of image, rebirth, and pride. No sense in doing things half-ass."

"Thank you, Frank."

"No problem. I'll speak with you on. . . ."

"But wait, Frank. There's more."

He took a deep breath and let it out. "Okay. Shoot."

"Some of the custodial crew are just along for the ride. I need real work. I need leverage."

"You've got it. Write up the goof-offs, and I'll do my best to put 'em someplace else. Same thing with the guards. You know Paterson. Nobody gets fired, people just get moved around."

"Frank, I could not do this without you behind me."

"Joe, we don't stand a chance at Eastside without you on the front line. Just get the job done."

Before the end of June, the Eastside High that had seemed so desolate was buzzing with the activity of renovation. The sandblaster scoured the outer walls, new windows were installed and the old windows were washed. Painters and plumbers, locksmiths and electricians, carpenters and masons, janitors with mops and buckets, janitors with waxers: all set to work. Trucks were always arriving, and dumpster after dumpster was filled with debris.

I saw to it that every worker wore an identification tag, and that each delivery person signed in at the guard's station and the office.

"Why are you doing this to me?" asked one truck driver.

"Sir, I am not doing this solely to you," I replied. "I am doing this to everyone. You need a good-working engine for your truck to run well, I need a good-working system for my school to run well. This practice of identification is a key part of my system— it keeps sludge out of the pistons, you might say—and it's going to stay in place as long as I am principal."

"You know, Mr. Clark," one of the custodial staff said to me on another occasion, "there is such a thing as good graffiti. Not this of course"—we were standing a few feet away from a wall that was being scrubbed to ready it for painting—"but some of it ain't bad."

"Harold, what you are calling good graffiti I call art, and yes, there is some worthwhile art in the modern mural category. In fact, come September I'm going to be checking out the students, searching for artistic natures to help me redecorate. It will be to Eastside's glory. But no one, Harold, no one is going to bring disrespect upon this institution and deface its appearance ever again without having to reckon with me."

As a shipment of desks arrived, I was talking with a woman who had just joined my administrative staff. We walked over to inspect the new material. One of the workers, pausing for a smoke, remarked, "That's one of the things they do at Rahway (the State Penitentiary). They assemble school desks."

"Sad to think," said the woman, "that some of these very desks might have been worked on by an ex-Eastsider."

"Sad indeed," said I. "I've often thought that some of the best minds of the black community end up in prison. They are clever, adventurous, brave, and magnanimous souls, many born leaders among them. But early on they are infected by the virulent and pervasive plague of the inner city, and soon, too soon, are irrevocably twisted, turn self-destructive, and become a plague to their people and their nation."

I paused. They were pulling the desks off the trailer, and lugging them past us into the building. "Mrs. Wilson," I said, "I want you to contemplate this as a primary goal of your new position."

"I'm not sure I follow you, sir."

"The reduction of the penitentiary population, Mrs. Wilson. Do not forget the bitter irony of these desks."

To make the building itself evoke respect, orderliness, decorum; to have it as a powerful and constant ally to my disciplined program for creating and maintaining an atmosphere conducive to learning—that's what this was all about.

I added amenities, because school, for all its necessary discipline, should never become drudgery. Rather, educators must carefully lead youths to the realization that the pursuit of a career is joyful and the acquisition of knowledge a delight. So, while banning ghetto blasters, I arranged for various forms of pop music to be played over the corridor loudspeakers. I had plants placed about the building, a fountain and a penny pond set in the main corridor, and couches put here and there in the corridors so that someone with a few minutes might relax and do a little extra studying or read a book.

I also spent hours establishing numerous new before-school and after-school programs and clubs, as well as drawing up themes for frequent assemblies and beginning the solicitations for a variety of guests. These efforts, which have since proven quite successful, were directed toward academic improvement, the building of self-esteem, the heightening of awareness of career possibilities, guidance and crisis assistance, and the development of scholastic, community, and civic pride.

My search for school artists yielded magnificent results. The clean and handsome appearance of the building was crowned that fall by numerous colorful, insightful, and inspirational works: murals, framed paintings, drawings, and posters. We have energetically maintained this practice to the present day. Whereas the chaotic and disgusting graffiti of Eastside B.C. was a sign of the incompetence of former administrators and the lawless spirit of the student body, the decorated halls of the new Eastside are patent testimony to our transformation.

One afternoon in early July, I strolled out to the property's perimeter to watch a work crew installing Eastside's new section of cyclone fence. It was there that the hoodlums had repeatedly ripped out patchwork repairs and reopened the gaping holes that gave them access to the school grounds. I was authorized by the superintendent to install a whole new section of sturdier chain-link to block their entry. While watching the metal poles being set in the ground, I looked up and noticed several individuals standing on the sidewalk about ten yards away, also observing the work. I had no trouble identifying them by their swaggering demeanors and scornful faces. Here were four dope-dealing thugs watching the erection of a new impediment to their business.

They had already fixed on me. We were suddenly staring at each other, staring hard. I stepped forward—into the breach, as it were—to the line where the fence would stand.

"Can I help you?" I called out, as sardonically as possible. "Do you fellows have some business with the high school?"

They were a little startled by my unexpected action. They talked among themselves. "Yeah, chief," one of them shouted back, "we're the health inspectors!"

They laughed, but my words quickly erased their smiles. "Then I suggest you quarantine yourselves."

It was hate staring at me then. "You a big smartass, ain't you?" one barked.

"That's right, chief. I've got more smarts in my ass than any drug addict's got in his brain. Now maybe you fellows would like to move along. There are some tools missing from this site. I am going in to report it. I imagine the police will be checking the persons of all suspects."

We were back to a silent staring match again, for a few moments. Then, at the whispered urgings of one, all four departed. But not before another pointed at me. "You, sucker," he said. "I'm gonna get you!"

I pointed right back. "Not if I get you first!"

"That's some pretty crazy stuff, principal," one of the workers said. The crew had naturally been watching this exchange. "Those lunatics are liable to come over and beat your ass."

"Nonsense. They're cowards. They saw your picks and shovels."

Another worker laughed. "But what made you think you could count on us to help you out?"

"Because you boys would have loved to break up the monotony by kicking some butt. Isn't that so?"

We got some laughs out of that. Of course, their presence alone had been a sufficient shield. But why did I speak up at all? Because I had to let the hoods know right from the start that I was not the least bit afraid of them. If I had simply stared and moved away, it would only have postponed our inevitable confrontation, and postponement was to their advantage. They might well have construed any passiveness as a sign of weakness, and certainly "the dude by the fence" would have been the subject of several rounds of group ridicule. Street life is like that. I know because I've lived it. But now, because of what did happen, they had to worry a bit about me. I could not simply be mocked for a wimp. Hell, "that dude" might even be crazy, liable to do anything. And if any Eastside student should hear the story, it might be a blow struck for education.

That same day, upon returning to the building, I summoned the custodian in charge. "Mr. Phillips, put aside what you're doing and give the display case a thorough cleaning."

"Yes sir, Mr. Clark."

"And has Guzman finished polishing the trophies?"

"Not yet, Mr. Clark. I had to assign him to cleanup in Room 204."

"Well, re-assign him back to the trophies. I want them thoroughly polished. I mean I want them to shine, Mr. Phillips. And I would like to arrange them in the display case before I go home this evening."

The school trophies had rarely been on display in the main corridor, because of fear that they would be stolen. As a result they had spent most of their time either in the principal's office or a dark closet. But what are trophies for if not for display? After confronting those miscreants it gave me special pleasure to set the statues and medals of Eastside's glory back in their glass cabinet.

"Mr. Phillips," I said, stepping back to admire the shiny array, "mark my words. There will not be another trophy stolen as long as I am principal."

"Yes sir, Mr. Clark." I dare say he was skeptical. But my prediction has, for seven years, been accurate.

Insight B
KEEPING MY TRAP SHUT

•

Before the school year opened in September, the Eastside teachers would never have swallowed my belief that we would achieve total victory in restoring order to Eastside High School. They would have found that notion incomprehensible, even weird.

That's why I did not reveal to them the total scope of my plans and did not tell them how the various details would mesh together to make everything succeed. The teachers were able to discern bits and pieces, but that's all. If I had let them in on too much of the plan, critics among them, especially the less visionary ones, would start whacking away at the details with the result that the entire plan could have been weakened. I told them only what they had to know.

Too often, an administrator kills or weakens a good plan by telegraphing in advance what he is going to do—instead of just doing it.

Look what happened to Richard Green, who became chancellor of New York City schools in 1988. Wishing to remove 30 principals he considered incompetent from their posts, and not being able to fire them (because of their union contract), he decided to kick them upstairs, at least getting them out of jobs where they would hurt education. It was a good idea, but he made one big mistake: He announced to the central board of education what he proposed to do.

Once the proposal was public the principals' union was up in arms against it. The teachers' union pledged solidarity. Green was advised that the threatened strikes would cripple the vast system at the very beginning of his first term. He withdrew the proposal.

Tactically, backing down at this point was wise. But as Wyatt Earp might have told him, and as Joe Clark definitely would have told him, Green should have shot first and asked questions later.

Each one of those principals could have, on one designated morning, been removed from his or her office by telling them something like, "We need you downtown this morning," and as soon as the duffer was out of the building, the replacement could have sat down at the desk and changed the nameplate. Certain voices would howl as soon as the purge was discovered, but the new principals would be in place. Despite the unions' outcry, the public and municipal officials would have welcomed and praised the *fait accompli*. Green would have been able to stand firm and carry out his plan, to the benefit of the students. As it is, the people Green wanted to move are still in their powerful positions.

4

THE TEAM

I REALIZED THAT I would have to get to know a lot of people even better than I knew the building.

Throughout that summer of 1982, I assiduously studied the resumes of every individual who would, come September, be working under me. I called every one of them in for an interview, doing this sometimes in groups and sometimes one-on-one, depending on what I needed to learn. I drew up a list of teachers who, it appeared, had been coasting. In September they would have to show a change of attitude and live up to their profession, or I would run them out, tenure or no tenure.

Very early in my planning I decided that the whole former administrative staff had to go. They were, when I thought of them collectively and of their namby-pamby nonfeasance, more obnoxious to me than the graffiti and the clogged urinals. Remarkably, even as I was drawing red lines through their names, I received a phone call from the former principal, my predecessor, who offered me his congratulations on my appointment.

"Thanks," I said, cordial as a hammer-rap.

He then, brazenly, offered to help pass on his legacy of failure by assisting me with my transition program.

"Thanks," I said. "I'll call if I need you."

"Please do. And Joe"—a blind man could have seen this one coming—"let me put in a good word for Mr. X. He's a loyal subordinate and an eminently capable administrator, and he knows Eastside thoroughly."

"I'm sorry, but I don't at all share your high regard for X."

"Aaa, umm, well. Then you should consider Mrs. Y. She'll be more to your liking. A bit more intelligent than X, and absolutely. . . ."

"Sorry. Can't use her."

"No? Aaa, aaa, well what about Z?"

"What about him?"

"Well, he'd be a fine, fine vice-principal, always there when you. . . ."

"Not my style. As a matter of fact, I think I'll bring in a whole new staff. My people."

"New . . . staff . . . your . . . aaa, well, umm, aaa, if I can at all be of any assistance whatsoever, you just. . . ."

"Thanks. I'll call if I need you. Have a restful summer. Good-bye."

I have a controversial way of choosing my administrative staff. I prefer women. I believe that, on the whole, women are more likely to see the sense in complete loyalty to me and my program. Men seem more worried about losing their identity in obedience, are more likely to covet the catbird seat, and to oppose me on some point or other solely for political reasons. None of which I need. Furthermore, I usually choose women who, on the average, have the fewest distractions, who can give me both time and devotion: that is, women with grown children, or women who are divorced or separated, or, ideally, women past menopause.

I can hear knees jerking and feminists gasping, but I emphatically believe that a principal owes it to his school to chose an administrative staff with whom he can work comfortably and get the job done. To each his own, and my staff must be mine.

There were two ironies, discernible only to myself, concerning my staff that first year. It did not, for one, turn out to be entirely new. I needed some people who were familiar with all the intricacies of Eastside administration. I chose two for their merit, neither among those recommended by my predecessor. The second irony was that two of my first vice-principals were men. I simply judged them to be dedicated individuals capable of constraining egotistical impulses in order to get the job done. One was a cool-headed administrator. He was one of the Eastside veterans and he had a record of efficiency. The other was a teacher and guidance counselor who had had no serious thoughts of entering the administrative field. While scouting for new blood, I had heard him praised by a person I trust, so I made inquiries and looked over his record. He was bright and self-effacing, a hard worker who combined compassion and discipline, and his students loved him. The first time we spoke was on the day I offered him the post. He was flabbergasted.

"But I have no experience, no training."

"You have enough experience," I replied. "As for training, just keep your mouth shut and watch me."

I knew I could count on the two women I chose. One had been my chief assistant at PS 6, and was as able as any administrator in the system. The other woman—the other veteran of Eastside—had distinguished herself as the head of the Science Department. *All four of those original vice-principals have gone on to become principals elsewhere.*

I met several times with my staff members before the school year began, both individually and as a group. I made each one responsible for at least two academic departments, and instructed each in how to work with and monitor their respective department heads.

"I have closely studied these chairpersons," I told them, "and have come to the conclusion that, though they have been appointed by the board, the department heads are, on the whole, dedicated and able individuals. Why else in the world would they wish to continue in such hard and thankless posts? This does not mean, however, that you vice-principals should not scrutinize their work. If a department head is acting wrongly or foolishly and I do not hear about it from the proper vice-principal, both your tails will feel the heat. Heads of departments are going to be appreciated and rewarded in this administration, just as long as they do their jobs. The same goes for you."

That, basically, is the management ladder. A teacher has recourse to the department head, the department head to the appropriate vice-principal, and the vice-principal to me. Simple structure, yes. But it works, and for three main reasons: good personnel who know they must perform or be ousted, an ardent principal who keeps everyone on his toes, and the added condition that anyone along that chain who does not feel that the problem is being fairly or adequately dealt with may come directly to me and I will deal with it.

"I will be here every day for anyone in the building or connected with the building," I told the staff. "During regular school hours the chain of command will be in effect and, unless there is a most dire emergency or I supersede the chain, it will be strictly adhered to. But in the mornings for two hours before classes, and after school, anyone may come directly to me. So, if you have a problem you feel will not be solved by going through the proper channels, wait and come to me. I, and you too, will emphasize this important option to everyone. The last thing an administrative staff should be is a wall for a so-called administrator to hide behind.

"One more thing. I want you accessible. I want you out patrolling the halls. I want you at least half as visible as I will be."

I divided up the other administrative tasks among them, and gave each some projects for the summer.

All the procedural aspects of my system were written down (by me) and handed out to staffers, secretaries, teachers, janitors, and guards. Almost every activity outside the classroom and inside the confines of Eastside had a proper and defined procedure: permissions, requisitions, meetings, assemblies, trips, disciplinary actions, special announcements, emergencies. I promised each teacher that as long as he or she did the job, he or she would have my full support.

"No more of the principal undermining a teacher's power by not enforcing discipline," I told a roomful of teachers in July. "And no more of a teacher failing to help a student in need because of administrative indifference."

"On the other hand," I added, "I did not write these rules of procedure because I am fond of paperwork. I am not. But I am fond of order, very fond in fact. I advise each and every one of you to study these rules, because they will be enforced without

exception. I assure you, this is not another paper tiger. It is a real
Bengal beast."

By August I was able to mail to my staff and teaching corps the
newly drawn up Eastside High School Suspension Policy for the
coming year. Which read as follows:

1. Fighting 10 days
2. Assault on Teacher (verbal or physical) 10 days
3. Drug or Alcohol Use 10 days
4. Selling of Drugs or Alcohol 10 days
5. Cafeteria
   a) Food Fights 10 days
   b) Failure to Remove Trays 10 days
6. Defacing of School Property
   a) Vandalism 10 days
   b) Graffiti 10 days
7. Carrying of Weapons 10 days
   This includes knives, guns or any item
   that could be used as a weapon
8. Defiance of Authority 10 days
9. Theft
   a) Personal 10 days
   b) School 10 days
10. Extortions—Muggings 10 days
11. Gambling 10 days
12. Arson 10 days
13. Socially Maladjusted Acts (Sex Offenses) 10 days
14. Actions that might cause physical harm to
    another person 10 days
15. Threatening Any Staff Member 5 days
16. Wearing of Hats 5 days
17. Profanity 5 days
    Whether in the classroom, cafeteria,
    auditorium, corridors, or gymnasium
18. In corridor without a pass 5 days
19. In building while on suspension 5 days

I noted that infractions 1–14 could result in expulsion, that
the principal reserves the right to suspend any student for an
infraction not listed, and that all penalties would be strictly
enforced. Each student received a copy on the first day of
classes, and duplicates were posted throughout the building.

"Hats?" piped one young male teacher, with thinly disguised ridicule. I had handed him the list following an interview.

I looked across the desk, into that sophomoric face. "You read the word correctly."

"Seriously, Mr. Clark. Do you really think the wearing of hats is something that merits discipline?"

"Do you think that teenage death is something that merits our concern?"

His grin froze. "I don't understand."

"As a teacher in an inner-city high school in the 1980s, you ought to."

The young man attempted to maintain his aplomb by leaning back in the chair and crossing his legs. While he was thus controlling his temper, I proceeded. "Ghetto youths have been murdered because of the hats they were wearing. Murdered because someone else desired the tall, silly leather thing or the big, colorful woven thing. And murdered because the hat identified the youth as a member of a particular gang."

"But no one has been murdered for a hat in Paterson," he said.

That was the last straw. My clenched fist came down hard on the desktop and I rose half out of my seat. "Goddammit, wake up! We are not dealing solely with Paterson. We are working within a complex economic, social, political, and cultural entanglement called the inner city, a deep entanglement that pervades the urban areas of this nation. And despite what some people would like to think, what goes on in the inner city has a direct effect on what happens in the rest of the country. Dope, crime, taxes, to give you some examples. Do you understand me?"

His legs were no longer crossed, but planted firmly on the floor. His hands gripped the arms of the chair. "Yes, Mr. Clark," he said. "Yes, I think I do."

"And in the inner city, youths get killed because of the hats they might be wearing. It has happened in Los Angeles, in Detroit, in Newark. Black and Hispanic youths cut down by their own kind before getting a chance at life. Maybe one was the next Washington Carver, or the next Neruda. And kids have been killed in Paterson, too, for reasons just as horribly absurd as a hat. Don't you think that we, as educators, ought to be concerned with the overtime work the Grim Reaper is doing among the home and neighborhood environments of our students?"

I re-took my seat. It was nice to see him blush, nice to know he was feeling some shame for his foolishness. "Yes, Mr. Clark, I do. I'm sorry."

"Don't apologize. I allow a teacher three mistakes. That was your first. You live in Fort Lee, don't you?"

That impressed him. Behold, a boss who actually reads resumes. "Yes, yes I do."

"Nice town. I live in South Orange, another pleasant area. But I grew up in Newark, smack in the heart of hell. And you and I work in another precinct of hell." I got up and led him to the door. "I know that you taught at Eastside last year, but let me suggest that, before you go home today to Fort Lee you take a drive around this neighborhood and remember where we are."

"I'll do that, Mr. Clark. I really do want to do a good job here."

"Glad to hear it. Because you will have to."

I also informed the teachers of my plan to make them my assistants for in-building security. This surprised and worried them. I presented them, as well, with a dress code, which was not universally appreciated.

"The grapevine is humming, Joe," said Frank Napier, stopping by in mid-August.

"And what's it saying?"

We were standing out in the hot day, admiring the big, clean building. Napier, smiling broadly, said, "They just don't know what to make of you, my friend. Oh, of course, they're impressed by the way you've cleaned up the building. Who the hell wouldn't be? And they admire your energy too. But there's a lot of the usual skepticism, and cynicism. People don't think anything good will ever happen here."

"People are often mistaken."

"I think they are this time. It's funny. Everybody's speculating on how much of a difference you'll make, on how much of you is just talk, on how long you'll last. But nobody seems to know what you've got planned."

"Because I haven't told anyone but you. Their ignorance is part of the plan. Let them get to know me through a big surprise, a one-day *coup d'etat*, or let them ridicule me as another crazy man."

He was thoughtful, gazing at the building. "You've got a real good chance, Joe," he said. "Keep those doped-up hoods out and you can make this thing work."

There was loud, disjointed music coming from down the block. "They're out for sure," I assured him. "They already know it. That's why they're sending me death-threats."

The superintendent looked at me with concern. "Already, eh. How many have you gotten?"

"Two."

We were eye to eye some moments. Hot, no wind. Slowly the smile returned to his face. "If you succeed," he said, "you'll get more."

I did.

5

WHAT WAS,
EXISTS NO MORE

BULLHORN IN HAND, I strode along the corridor, looking calm, but inwardly excited about this my debut as Eastside's principal. My mind flashed to what had happened on the first day of classes the previous year, 1981. A hoodlum with a switchblade had stabbed a guard who was trying to break up a drug deal. The wound was not fatal. But that brutal act set the tone for the rest of the school year—largely because the stabbing did not lead to a strong, rigorously enforced code of discipline. I was determined that a more impressive deed, this one by legitimate authority, was going to set a different and better tone on this opening day.

I paused in the corridors and looked around. Everything clean, orderly, ready. The revived woodwork gleamed. The buffed floors shone. The resurrected trophies sparkled. The school looked better than many (too many) of the houses where Eastside students had risen that morning.

The teachers were milling about and chatting. We were still ten minutes away from the time the students would be entering the building. The teachers were cordial enough to me, but I could feel the tension on every side, and see the skepticism in their eyes.

Most of them had seen Eastside High eat a few principals, and more than a few teachers. Among the teachers, there was not a lot of faith in "the new guy." Some of the scuttlebutt had me as a martinet with a giant ego and a bunch of weird ideas. Some coasters wanted me to fail. Other teachers, who saw and appreciated the transformation I had carried out on the building, were willing to give me a chance, to wait and see if any good might come of these efforts. But their minds, too, were tinged with the prevailing pessimism.

I had no illusions. There would be no honeymoon period. A first day *coup d' etat*, from which there would be no turning back, was essential. And it would, indeed, be a *coup d'etat*, a toppling from power. In the past it was the kids who ran Eastside. They had the power. They set the tone, and the tone they set was chaos. They acted, and administrators reacted. Very soon, power at Eastside would change hands. All education, I reflected, depends on communication: the message sent, the message received. In a few short minutes I would be sending a message—to the students, the teachers, the staff, the hoodlums, the parents, the whole town—a loud and clear message about that indispensable condition for education—order—and the discipline necessary to achieve it. Education was about to recommence at Eastside High.

Two minutes to curtain. I raised the bullhorn to my lips. "Teachers," I announced, "assume your positions."

They assuredly did not like that. As I strode to the main entrance I caught some grimaces and glares, detected some muttering. But the teachers adhered to the new "weird" rule, each stepping to the center of the corridor, opposite his or her classroom door. I suppressed a smile and wondered if any of them had the purposely withheld reason for this arrangement. Let 'em gripe. They would know soon enough.

At 8:30 A.M., I was standing at the top of the stairs, just inside the main entrance. As the students in a steady flow pushed through the doors and mounted the steps, I used the bullhorn to declare:

"I am your new principal, Joe Clark. Mr. Clark to you. This is the new Eastside High School. What was, exists no more. Go to your classrooms. Please walk to the right."

I met the eyes of the first bunch of kids through the door. There was surprise and wonderment in face after face. Their principal had never greeted them before. Eastside youths who had never been sent to the office for misconduct had almost never even seen their principal before. Now they saw him: a lean man in a three-piece suit, standing like a drill sergeant, wielding a bull-horn, looking serious business. There was an almost imperceptible pause among that first group—as though an animal psyche was asking itself whether or not to challenge this stranger—then they moved forward, quietly, dividing into two streams for two corridors, obeying without a hitch or grumble the directive to walk along the right.

More kids flowed in, followed along in orderly fashion. I repeated the message periodically, until every member of the three upper classes (freshmen were to report later that opening day) had come face to face with the new principal, and had filed along accordingly.

Now and again I took a look at the teachers. Their expressions showed more amazement than those of the students, as if they were seeing magic. The student body, which in previous years rumbled through the corridors like a buffalo stampede, had suddenly been transformed into a model of orderliness. And they, the teachers, were participating in the magic, like unwitting volunteers a magician has plucked from the audience. Each teacher, by standing in the center of the corridor, served as a clear demarcation post, signaling the channel for student traffic, which moved always along the right, up and down the halls, throughout the building.

No Eastside teacher ever griped again about standing in mid-corridor between classes. For teacher, student, and administrator, the tone was set for the rest of the year, and indeed for the new Eastside ever since—the calm, firm tone of order.

More magic was performed at noon when the freshmen arrived. Traditionally (B.C.) these kids were promptly treated to their own special helping of the confusion that permeated the place. They were crowded haphazardly into the auditorium, where each teacher assigned to a freshman homeroom would, one after another, stand before them and read the list of names of his or her students. This tiresome procedure usually devoured the rest of the day. It also killed off the last iota of patience in a good many teachers, who found themselves shouting unfamiliar names into a noisy mob of kids, who, having noticed the lack of order and authority, were gleefully diving into the pandemonium.

I learned of this foolishness that summer when I asked a teacher her main complaints about the *ancien regime*. High on the list was the pitiful organizing of the freshman class.

"I almost quit last year, on the very first day," she said, her eyes wide. "And I'm a ten-year veteran. I mean, the first thing I did when we finally got to the homeroom, was to write out my resignation. I really don't know what kept me from handing it in. I know one thing, though: I did not feel like teaching anyone anything for over a week. And any time I think of going through that ordeal again I think of quitting."

I did not, at first, reply—my mind was already wrestling with the problem. She, feeling awkward because of the silence, blushed and lowered her head. "Perhaps you do not think it such a big thing. But that kind of experience on the first day dashes one's hopes for anything turning out right."

"On the contrary," I said at last. "I consider this quite a big thing, and I here and now guarantee you that I will rectify the situation. From now on, no good teacher is going to want to quit Eastside High. As for bad teachers, that is an entirely different story. They are going to feel the fire at their heels and want to flee."

It's like the tale of Columbus and the egg. After Columbus made his historic voyage and was back in the court of Queen Isabella, several of Spain's naval bigshots were minimizing his great deed, claiming that there was really little navigational skill involved in sailing due west, and that any one of them could have done it as well, and probably better. So Columbus got a hard-boiled egg from the royal kitchen and challenged any one of the admirals to make the egg stand upright in the palm of the hand. Each tried and each failed. They claimed it was impossible, and sneered when Columbus said he could do it easily.

He took out his knife, sliced off the bottom, and stood the egg up in his palm. "That's cheating," the admirals complained. "That's just too simple. Anyone could have done that."

"Yes," said Columbus, "anyone could have. But it was I alone who thought of it, and I alone who did it."

That story could apply to many reforms I instituted at Eastside, including my program for making the corridors orderly. It particularly applies to my plan for organizing the incoming freshmen into classes.

When the freshmen arrived that day, they were told to proceed (moving along the right side, of course) to the cafeteria, where more than 20 tables had been arranged. Each table was designated by a letter of the alphabet. On the table with the first letter of the student's last name, that student found a list that included his or her name, the name of the new homeroom teacher, and instructions to proceed to the auditorium. The teacher arrived, announced only one name, his or her own, and the students of that homeroom class assembled and followed the teacher out. Time and aggravation were cut to a minimum. Teachers were, on the whole, astounded and appreciative. Yet there was some talk about how anyone could have thought of it—though for 20 years no one had. Break out the hard-boiled eggs.

Whatever those freshmen had heard about Eastside—and they had heard plenty—was greatly discredited by that calm and orderly first day. Yes, people were about to start hearing much different news concerning Eastside High.

Insight C
HOW I KEPT THE PUSHERS OUT
•

A spectacle is always impressive. The calm, orderly atmosphere of the first day of school was certainly a spectacle, because it was so radically different from Eastside past, and everyone was astonished. At the same time, something else was operating. It was less visible but every bit as significant. That first day marked the end of the booming Eastside High School open-air, cash and carry drug market. I had planned it that way, and many of the things I had done over the summer were aimed specifically at shutting down the drug business . . . permanently.

The best way to get drugs out of a school is to keep them from getting in. My program for keeping drugs out involved making the school a fortress that pushers couldn't penetrate. The specifics included:

- Replacing the weak fence of old with the serious, no-nonsense fence.
- Repairing the door locks. Then we made it our business to learn which students would be likely to help drug pushers by opening the doors from the inside and letting them in. We kept a very sharp eye on those kids.
- Replacing one ineffective layer of security with two effective layers. In the past, the 18 security guards did whatever they did inside the building. They certainly didn't do very much because non-student hoodlums entered the building at will, and their business was thriving.

My plan called for stationing the guards outside the building, to serve as a perimeter defense. They would guard the gates, the grounds, the doors. A lot of teachers groused about that over the summer. They feared that because the inside of the building would be guardless, I was throwing them to the wild student mob, which would most certainly devour them—and then have me and my policies for dessert. They also complained that it was extra duty.

Because I had decided not to justify my plans to the

teachers ahead of time, my only response to their complaints was to remind them who was principal.

Under my plan, the teachers themselves and the administrators would be the in-school security. (And, as I knew it would, the system worked.) The teachers, who stood in the corridors before school and between class periods, plus roving administrators, proved to be security a-plenty. (Obviously, various aspects of my plan were interrelated. The teachers and administrators were an effective indoor security force partly because thugs couldn't get into the building any more, and partly because of everything I did to establish the new tone of calm and orderliness.)

- Sending the punks a message. I did this by appointing Stephen Brown to be my special assistant for discipline. The hoods knew who he was. He had been the only obstacle they had to contend with in previous years.

Brown is a history teacher who used to play football for the New York Giants. He's big, fearless, and dedicated to the well-being of his students. He was the only real security force the previous administration had. Because he had the reputation as the only person who could stop hoods, the administration assigned him to the classroom adjacent to the side entrance where the hoods of the B.C. era often entered, because from there it was only a quick dart to the cafeteria. Brown detested the drug dealers and their sinister activities, so during class he would leave his classroom door open. When he heard activity in the stairwell area, he would investigate. He often found himself wrestling with three or four hoods.

It is a wonder that he wasn't knifed or shot. I was outraged when I learned that, instead of stationing a guard at that door, the administration kept Brown there to police that dangerous area, not only distracting him from his proper job, teaching history, but also placing his life in jeopardy.

Appointing Brown to the discipline position was one of my first acts. It was partly symbolic—to send a message to the hoods. So I publicized the move. In my first bulletin to the faculty and students, I ran a photo of Brown and announced his new role. I knew the punks would see it, and I knew it would give them something to think about.

- Setting up a thorough, rigorously maintained ID card system. The students were photographed the first day of school, and in about two weeks the cards were distributed.

Other Eastside principals had tried ID card systems in the past, but, because of slack enforcement, they never lasted longer than a few weeks. By the time our system started, there was no doubt that it would last, because by then there was no doubt that I would enforce every rule.

I made it clear that the laminated photo cards had to be worn at all times. I made the card a form of collateral for a hall or lavatory pass, or for the use of certain equipment. I made lending it or altering it serious offenses. Suspended students had to give up their cards. Anyone who forgot his or her card had to see me to be issued a substitute. Anyone who lost the card had to pay for another. I even saw to it that there were different colored dots on different cards, denoting lunch periods, so no unwarranted students, could hang around the cafeteria unnoticed.

Of course, all other school personnel have to wear IDs, and each visitor must wear an authorized pass. The system worked beautifully, making teachers' and administrators' monitoring duties much easier. They can spot people who don't belong in the school. The system is still in effect.

The result of all this, of course, is that the drug dealers have been permanently shut out from Eastside High.

6

LESSONS FOR TEACHERS

THE TEACHERS ENTERED the auditorium, in ones, twos, or in bunches, and took seats near the stage. We were almost halfway through my first year as Eastside's principal, and I thought a teacher assembly was in order.

Though the positive evidence had been accumulating since the first day of school, it took several weeks before the majority of the teachers were willing to concede that a significant change had been brought about and a new order established. First it was ascribed to luck—a one-day wonder, a two-day fluke—then to a blustery facade which was sure to crack and reveal walls of straw. But the transformation held, settled in, strengthened on all fronts as time went on. Threats and verbal and physical abuse against teachers ended. Vandalism against their property and school property ceased, utterly. Drugs, alcohol, and sexual assaults had disappeared from the school. The chaos in the halls between classes and the disruptive wildness of hoodlums in the corridors during classes, which had been an everyday occurrence in days past, vanished. For the first time in 20 years the corridors of Eastside were quiet. Teachers began to unlock and

54

open their doors during class. It is a practice that has endured to this day.

But on that afternoon, despite the obvious progress, I was still an unknown commodity to many of the teachers. I was (and unabashedly am) such a stickler for discipline and detail that many who encountered the same Joe Clark every day must have supposed me to be wound too tightly, therefore ready to snap and do something really stupid or crazy. At least a few, whose scams I was on to, were hoping for no less. I smiled, as the seats filled up, to think how disappointed they would be, then went forward with my intention to let all the teachers become a little more acquainted with their principal.

Standing downstage and speaking without a microphone, I said, "I would like any teacher into whose classroom I have made at least one unexpected visit to stand up."

No one, for a moment, moved, except to glance around a bit nervously. Teachers were apprehensive, I reckon, that the new principal meant to embarrass them before their peers. Finally one woman rose, then another, then a man. Then two more teachers got up, and the next second five more. Then, amid smiles and blushes, scores of teachers rose, until about 200 of Eastside's 250 teachers were on their feet.

Soon afterwards I learned that almost all of these teachers had not mentioned to their colleagues that I had dropped by. Many felt that my visit was prompted by some rumor or behind-the-back report of an impropriety or inadequacy, so they had kept quiet about my visit in an attempt to defer further scrutiny.

"Apparently very few of you took me seriously when I told you that I was going to be ubiquitous," I said. "Now perhaps you know better. Your distrust is, however, understandable. I suspect that most of you have never before worked under a real principal. Yes, you are being monitored, but you are also being supported in your labors. Do your jobs, obey the rules, and you will find you have in me your staunchest ally."

I went on to speak of the significant transformation that had already occurred at Eastside, and spent some minutes on how teacher-student relations had improved. "I remember how worried many of you were about my stationing of the guards outside the building. You thought your safety was threatened. You thought it would prove too onerous a task for the principal and his teachers to make up the in-building security team. But now you see how things have gone. You see the order and the calm that reign within these halls, and you are happy for this new situation. Something else has happened, too, because of my placing the guards outside. Your bond with your students has become stronger, and promises to grow stronger still. The guards had always been intruders. They could never really have been anything else. They were in the building because order had broken down. The unspoken message of their presence was, and could always only be, that the adults, we adults, had failed to make education happen here. We must never fool ourselves and think that unspoken messages like that are ever lost on the young. When the message is the opposite—which now it is—it comes through even clearer, because the human mind is better disposed to good news. It is good news, teachers, that the adults are again in control of the building. The students are able to respect you now. They can listen to, and learn from, someone they respect.

"The essential equation for learning is that the student be able to receive what the teacher is transmitting. Without order and calm, learning cannot happen. Without mutual respect, learning cannot happen. And what we must not forget is that learning, an education, is what the great majority of these kids want, and they do not mind the discipline it takes to get one.

"You teachers want to teach. Now you can."

From the start among the teachers there had been some grousing about my insistence on a system of specific duties—promptitude and precision, written passes, strict chain of command, and so forth—but most of the opposition died away as the system effectively proved itself. However, there were several people calling themselves teachers who had, quite rightly, recognized me as a threat to their less-than-professional routines. They saw it to their advantage to do all they could to derail my program of reform. Early on this handful of dodgers latched onto the issue of my teacher dress code as an instrument for cutting me down.

I issued an order that male teachers must wear ties and jackets, and that female teachers wear dresses or proper suits. I outlawed jeans, sweatpants, sneakers, and sandals. As with my other new regulations, teachers who might not have particularly cared for the dress code reluctantly adhered to it, and eventually saw the sense of it.

That is, except for these several. They complained that it was against their civil rights to be forced to wear a tie and sportscoat. The term in the contract was "appropriate attire," and there had been endless argument over who decided what constituted appropriate attire. I appeared powerless because these teachers were tenured and could not be fired. (The key word in the previous sentence is "appeared.") I advised the recalcitrant teachers to apply for transfers, and let it be known that the superintendent, upon my request, was willing to grant them, in order to keep the peace and not jeopardize the revival we were accomplishing at Eastside. But they (at first, at any rate) refused.

"Oh no!" one man, who was a particular nuisance, shouted at me. "I'm staying right here, and wearing what I like. You can't push me around. I know my rights."

"And I know how to do what must be done!" I roared, furious. We were alone in the conference room, glaring at each other. I roared on, as he fumed and tried several times to interrupt. "I have had my eye on you from the start. Your resume suggests it, and your performance proves it. You are a coaster, a parasite. You don't give a tinker's damn about the kids here or about education. All teaching means to you is a way to make money without really working."

"Go ahead, say what you like! You're frustrated because you can't move me. I've got rights!"

"I know. You're a protected loafer. But you just aren't protected enough to stop me." I leaned close. We were eyeball to eyeball. "Because I am after you and I am going to get you. I never start a war I can't win. This war has started and you are going to lose. I'm going to be in your face every time you turn around. I am relentless, mister, relentless. You will be out of this school, I guarantee it. You will either leave under your own volition, or they will carry you out in a straitjacket!"

I inaugurated a war of attrition against this coasting gang. I was in their faces, often. Much too often for their liking. I checked each of their attendance sheets, each of their lesson plans, personally. It was not at all difficult to find things amiss, especially in the lesson plans, which were full of grammatical errors and sloppiness of concept. Though I was not above twisting the screws on them, they made my mission easy simply by being the duffers they were. I demanded re-writes upon re-writes. I was forever observing their classes, and forever summoning them for conferences, at which the topic would be something like their probable inability to teach cod how to swim. I cut deeper, upbraiding them before their students, and in the teeming corridors, exposing their incompetence for all to see. Hard tactics, yes, but what choice had I? Let a few parasites corrode the structure of a fine teaching corps and maliciously laugh in the face of my reforms simply because they had hung around an inner-city cesspit of a school (Eastside B.C.) long enough to get tenure? Hell no.

"This is harassment!" one cried.

"Sue me."

"You are being totally unprofessional," I was informed by another.

"My profession is the administration of this school, which means I must do all I can to promote the right education of the students. Getting rid of a leech like you would promote education markedly."

Eventually their resistance wore down. One by one the troublesome few applied for, and received, transfers. It's a shame, really, that knavish, incompetent teachers cannot be fired outright, but are permitted—under union protection—to pollute the youth at another school. I personally would much rather fire someone, or write him or her up for the superintendent to fire, then use all that energy to get the person transferred. It is time we Americans began to rethink this notion of tenure—for principals as well as for teachers.

"I am prescribing this dress code," I said to an earlier assembly of teachers, "because I want everyone to project an image of dignity, self-respect, and professionalism. As educators, our first responsibility is to the students. Consequently, we must keep in mind the nature of the kids we're dealing with. They are ghetto kids who, if not reached by us, are misled by the false wisdom of the street. If you are dressed sloppily and seem like you don't care about yourself, you will not reach them. They are going to take you for a joke and a fool, and, by extension, to think that the knowledge you are offering is worthless, because it apparently hasn't helped you to dig yourself. Their assessments might not be valid, but that is what they will think.

"These youths desire, and are ready for, role models, but will reject someone who seems to lack self-respect. They want to look up to someone, someone they feel has overcome the problems they are facing. I assure you, teachers, this is not a neutral situation. Many of them have given up looking to their parents. Often we are their only decent choice. If they reject us as role models, they will readily choose the drug dealer in the fur coat and gold chains. I implore you not to turn from this responsibility, but graciously accept it as part of a teacher's territory. You see, I am intent on doing all I humanly can to give these disadvantaged youths a fair chance at education, which means a fair chance at life. Work with me in keeping this goal uppermost. Recognize that I need your cooperation, which is to say your professional loyalty, to make my intention a reality."

But the appeal for professional loyalty, which included strict adherence to my rules of procedure, was lost on several individuals who, doing their own things, ran, naturally, smack into me. There was one such collision that the film *Lean on Me* has popularized. But the whole story was not told in the movie.

We had a talented music teacher who paid little heed to the procedures and regulations I expected everyone to follow. Without filling out a request form or telling her department head or any administrator, she commissioned a photographer to take a picture of her class, with the intention of sending the school the bill. She also tried billing the school for an unrequested, unauthorized trip for her class. In both cases I would have approved and the school would have paid, if she had only gone through the proper channels.

She waltzed into the main office and made unauthorized use of the PA system—something no other teacher or staffer has done—when all she had to do was relay the message to me or a vice-principal. She moved her class through the halls, again without permission or passes, to use the auditorium, without a thought as to whether someone else might be using it. To have 20 students moving around without passes—20 students who would surely tell their friends that Joe Clark's rules did not apply in their case—was the sort of bad example guaranteed to erode

Eastside's hard-won discipline if allowed to continue. But when I brought this up to her, she acted as though she did not know what I meant.

My standing policy regarding insubordination is "three strikes, you're out," and rarely have I said more to a staffer or teacher than "That's one." In her case, because she was a good teacher, I let the count run to seven or eight strikes. But, finally, order had to be defended.

When—once again without request or approval or even a mention to anyone—she invited members of an opera company to come lecture and sing to her class, I requested her transfer. Rather than go elsewhere in Paterson, she left the system. I could not let all I worked for be undermined by one person's whims.

Teaching is not a bad career. There are challenges, benefits, opportunities for advancement, even for self-fulfillment. It beats a lot of other jobs. The pay, however, is less than what good teachers deserve, and the job security is better than what bad teachers should be allowed to have. But because of the pay, and of the battle-zone that inner-city schools have become, many able individuals turn to more lucrative, if less morally rewarding, careers. On the other hand, because the job security is unreasonably good, and the pay not all that bad, many individuals with little or no inner desire to educate anyone, including themselves, idle their way into teaching. I have a duty to keep such people away from the students.

One afternoon, while stalking the halls, I stopped outside the door of an English class taught by a new teacher, a young woman. She had written some words on the board. Vocabulary is one of my passions. I stepped inside. "Those are some very fine words," I remarked. She seemed a little nervous. She smiled. "Perhaps some of your students know the meanings?"

I asked one student what "tenacious" meant. "I don't know, Mr. Clark," she said.

"Does anyone?" I asked. No hands. "Does anyone know what 'mendicant' means?" No hands. "How about 'deride'?" Nothing. " 'Alacrity'? Does any student know the meaning of 'alacrity'? No? Very well. You will all soon learn these definitions, so listen carefully."

I turned to the teacher and asked her to define "alacrity" for the class. She stared at me in silence for some moments. Nervous, I thought. But she has to develop a good classroom manner. "Well," I said, "what are you waiting for? Give the class the definition."

She rubbed her hands, shuffled her feet. " 'Alacrity,' " she muttered. "Aaaa, aaa. . . ." More shuffling, wringing her hands now. Her face turned ashen. In the long, tense silence it dawned on me.

"You don't know what the word means?" I said. She said nothing. I bridled, I thundered. "You don't know what the word means?"

She hung her head, and said, "No."

"This is an outrage! You are not a teacher! No one can teach what they do not know. You are a disgrace! Out! Out of this classroom! Go to my office!"

I soon taught that tenure-seeking dolt the meaning of 'alacrity.' She was out of a job with plenty of it.

The next time I noticed a list of words on a classroom board I did not hesitate to step inside. " 'Synopsis,' Mrs. McCabe," I said, "you cannot expect these freshmen to know the meaning of words like 'synopsis.' "

"It means summary, Mr. Clark," said the first youth to raise a hand.

I smiled. It felt good to be wrong, knowing that a teacher was doing her job, and that learning was taking place. I stepped out of the room, stood a moment in the quiet corridor, smiled again.

There was also an assistant coach who figured he'd teach his social studies class in coach's shirt and tennis shoes. I sent him home. He cursed and ranted. He came back with a letter from the Board of Education stating that I could not throw him out. I read the letter, and once again told him to leave. When I reached for his arm to escort him to the door, he started bellowing that I had hit him. He filed suit. The only problem with his story was that a half dozen people plainly saw him not get hit. He lost his case, and his post at Eastside.

I demand a lot from my teachers. It's my duty to do so, my duty to the students. It is also part of my duty to the students, and to the furtherance of education, to get along with the teachers, so I work at doing that, too. I do not let jobs well done go uncommended. And when I throw them a party at Christmas or school year's end, I don't attend, so they can have if they want, the added bonus of bashing the boss.

One year I surprised the teaching corps by asking what I could do for them. They huddled for a while but couldn't come up with anything they needed, which I took as pretty good testimony that I had been doing my job. Finally somebody said that the teachers' lounge needed a fresh coat of paint. It got one the following day.

Says Henry Baker, a gym instructor, who was at Eastside B.C. and is still there today:

"The common cry of the troublemaker in those years before Clark was 'Go ahead, send me to the principal,' because he knew nothing would happen. There were rules then, of course, but they just weren't enforced. The principal was not behind us, but was concerned with not making waves—he did not want to antagonize anyone, is what he said—which only caused more trouble and disorder, because kids who should have been disciplined just weren't. Then Clark, who is an organizer and a fair man, came in with a plan, and turned everything around. He has restored order and discipline. Nobody wants to go to the principal now. Kids will be kids, there will always be some fooling around. But now they realize that there are limits, that if you cross a certain line there will be unpleasant consequences. Clark's policy keeps the kids within bounds, and that makes a teacher's job so much easier."

Says Florence Lopas, a Spanish teacher and the head of the Foreign Language Department:

"Before Clark I would come to school reluctantly, with an ache in my gut, thinking 'What's it going to be today?' Since Clark, work is fun again. Time flies by. Because we are doing the jobs we love, and that's because his method, which he makes work with his brain and his energy, is allowing us to."

I am not merely using some teachers to pat myself on the back. Rather, I am making the point that, within the parameters of my system, and despite the occasional weeding out that the union and the local media like to make much of, teachers have found at the new Eastside an atmosphere conducive to teaching. Which means an atmosphere conducive to learning, which is what it is all about.

In 1985, the teachers of Paterson struck for higher salaries. I am not pro-union, but I am pro-teacher, and I knew that my dedicated corps of instructors deserved a raise. Indeed, they deserved, and still do, more than they thought prudent to ask for. The media came out to Eastside, expecting Crazy Joe Clark to be railing against the teachers and the union. Weren't they surprised to learn that I supported the strike. Nonetheless, they got their flashy story. A teacher crossed the picket line, came to the front door, demanding entry.

I met him there. "So," I said, "you actually want to work today?"

"Yes. It's my right."

"Very well." I reached inside the door, dragged out a chair I had made ready for just such an occasion, and set it down on the outer landing, in full view of picketers and media personnel. "Sit here today if you want to work," said I. "No one is allowed inside."

I, like everyone else, was astonished when he actually did sit down. He wanted to make his point, or draw his pay, or whatever it was. The picketers started to ridicule him. The photographers started snapping pictures. Finally he got up and went home. The chair became known as the scab chair. I became known as supportive of my teachers. Rightly so, from day one, and about time people realized it. Supportive of my teachers and of my students. Supportive of education.

Insight D
HE'S EVERYWHERE
•

Research has shown that the single most important ingredient for the success of a school is the principal. And I feel that to be successful a principal must be a benevolent Big Brother. Like Big Brother, the principal should be all-knowing and ubiquitous. And the only way a principal can be all-knowing is by being ubiquitous.

Therefore, during school hours I am almost never in my office for more than a few brief minutes at a time. The principal's office isn't the place where education happens. So I'm always on the prowl—in the corridors, in the classrooms, in the gym, on the stairs, everywhere.

Someone once attached a pedometer to me and we learned that on an average day, just walking around the school, I cover 22 miles.

It is only by being out amongst 'em that a principal learns what is really going on in the school. By roaming the school, I learn:

• Who the kids are and what they're thinking.
• Who is a good teacher and who is not.
• What undercurrents could develop into a serious problem.
• What problems the teachers face.
• What the status is of every inch of the physical plant. If anything is amiss, I spot it.
• What programs are working and which ones are not.
• How well staff people are doing their jobs.

In addition to seeing, I want to be seen. I want students and teachers always to be aware of Joe Clark, and to know that I care about every single detail of Eastside High School. I want people to think, "He's everywhere."

My constant physical presence is also a reminder of my disciplinary code. At Eastside B.C., in the days of invisible principals, the security guards were supposed to be the visible reminders of discipline. Hah! In those days, when a bunch of kids who were up to something spotted a roving security guard approaching, they'd shrug and say, "Let's go hide for a minute. He'll never catch us. Even if he does, so what. Nothin' will come of it." And they were right. They knew that no guard would be in a hurry to nab thugs who might hurt him. They knew that guard would get his pay whether he ran after them or walked after them.

But when they see Joe Clark coming, well that's different. They say, "We're done for! He'll catch us no matter where we hide, and suspend us, or have us arrested, or both." They know Joe Clark will chase them and track them down, because he wants his school de-leechified more than he wants his paycheck.

In addition to being seen, it is important for a principal to be heard.

The bullhorn has become my trademark. At school, I *always* carry it. It is a magnificent device for transmitting and magnifying the voice of authority. It is also useful for such mundane things as hailing people and prodding slow hallway traffic. Ever since my bullhorn and I began getting national media attention, other principals around the country have started toting bullhorns.

Because of physical limitations that I do not like to admit to, I cannot actually be everywhere at once. But by effective use of the bullhorn and the public address system, I can give the *illusion* of being everywhere. One such technique is to bellow over the PA. I do that because what I say is important. It's been said that when I talk over the PA system I sound like the Wizard of Oz. Good.

7

ATTENTION ALL PARENTS! REPORT TO YOUR POSTS!

A WHILE AGO, I received word of a hookey party in progress. Scores of Eastside students were partying at a house in the neighborhood.

I notified the police, but I made it a point to arrive on the scene before them, armed with my bullhorn. If kids thought I was ubiquitous in the corridors of the school, I smile to think what went through their minds when they heard my unmistakable voice booming outside that house. "Oh, no! Clark! Here!" What a commotion ensued. Kids bolting in every which way, out every door and window, scurrying like squirrels. Some got away. But a large number surrendered *en masse*. The tale of my escapade instantly spread all over town.

Which, of course, is what I wanted it to do. I wanted to make a large impression, one of folkloric proportions if possible, upon the youths and upon their parents. The message for the parents was to get serious about your children getting to school and acquiring their educations. The message got through. Now the phone in the attendance office rings with much more regularity.

Parents need to be reminded periodically just how important

education is. A principal, through his deeds, should keep re-
minding them. When I took this job I knew it would be a war,
and knew that the parents, if I could rouse them, were my
natural allies.

That thought flashed in my mind while, on a November night
in 1982, I watched a solitary woman at a microphone. Behind
her, seated at the long table, were the nine members of the
Paterson Board of Education. I was amused at the amazement on
the faces of the board members. What astonished them was the
fact that they were looking out on a meeting-room packed to the
doorways with concerned and vocal parents, my supporters,
who had come out in force on a cold weeknight, and *only two
months into the first year of my Eastside administration*, to
defend their children's principal from the official complaint and
verbal attack of one mother.

The usual room for Board of Education meetings, with a capacity for approximately 100 people, proved far too inadequate
for this large turnout. The startled officials had to move the
meeting to a room at City Hall. All told, 500 or more parents
showed up in my support. A grand total of one—no exaggeration—was there in opposition.

At issue was the well-considered and absolute dismissal of
approximately 300 so-called students from Eastside High. I did
it by using my executive prerogative of meting out indefinite
(which is to say, permanent) suspension. It was expulsion, in
fact, and everyone knew it, though technically a Paterson principal is not empowered to expel anyone. But any real leader has to
be ready to stretch the boundaries of his position, when it be-
comes clear that doing so will help him accomplish a good
objective. My objective is to shape an environment conducive to
education. I inherited a student body shot through with the
diseases of the ghetto and the street, an infected student body in
need of a serious purge.

In the first six weeks of my first year at the helm, I intensely
studied the student body. Actually, I had begun the scrutiny
during the Summer, staying up late with student records and, by
September, had a good idea of which young people merited
particular observation. I was able to distinguish an incorrigible
core of youths who were students in name only. They were
recalcitrants and recidivists who loved disorder and promoted it

every day. They would have welcomed back the thugs and drug dealers. Their receptiveness to learning was all but non-existent, and their presence in the classrooms cried out for some sort of alternative program. It was shortly after I became the principal that my first appeal went out to the Board of Education, beseeching it to set up alternative schools for both the social deviants and those with learning disabilities. The board did nothing. These people were the ones I weeded out.

One mother protested, and could recruit no one to join her protest. Where were all the other parents? Well, they either did not know (possible, but unlikely); or had to work (doubtlessly true for many); or they (a tragically large percent, I fear) did not care. But I think the largest percentage of those absent parents agreed with the logic of my decision, if not with the decision itself, and were thus ashamed to show their faces.

"Joe Clark is our man!" "He saved Eastside!" "Our kids need Clark!"—that's what the voices and the placards were shouting that November night.

"Thank you very much." That's what the chairman of the Board of Education said to that solitary woman, after she had lodged her complaint and said her piece. That's all the board ever said and ever did concerning this matter. If any member doubted the rightness of what I had done—there were a few members who agreed with me—he or she certainly could not have doubted the powerful, near universal support I was receiving. No board member had ever witnessed—except, perhaps, after a rape, stabbing, or other heinous crime had been committed in one of the schools—such a huge congregation of concerned parents.*

Those 500 parents were there for me because I had every day been there for their children. Barely two months had elapsed, yet those parents who did not know me, certainly knew of me. They would ride past the school, see the cleanliness, and spot signs of the new discipline. They would hear from area store owners of the kids' improved behavior. In complete contrast to my predecessors, I was (and still am) a visible, accessible principal. I seized any opportunity I had to meet a youngster's parents.

* Five years later, when both my reputation and the envy of several board members had increased, there was a big flap over another group suspension. I describe that incident in Chapter 10.

And I let it be known that any parents wishing to speak with me about any matter connected with their child's education was encouraged to do so. I still hold to this sound policy, and I arrive at the building before sunrise to speak with parents on the phone and in person for two hours before the first bell. Also, members of my staff and of the Guidance Department are instructed to make themselves accessible to any parent wanting to talk.

In some cases, my reputation helped garner support. I had been the principal at PS 6 who had performed "The Miracle on Carroll Street," returning discipline and academic accomplishment to Paterson's chief grammar school version of Eastside B.C. I worked that "miracle" by using that same magic of analysis and appropriate action, involving managerial skill, persistence, and guts. I went against the grain of a decadent liberal policy. For more than a decade delinquent administrators and teachers had simply been passing untaught kids along to the next grade level. The first year at PS 6 I kept 400 pupils back; the next year more than 300. I refused to allow any teacher of mine to promote an undeserving student.

"It ought to be damned evident to you, and to everyone else," I remember forcefully informing one teacher, who wondered if we were being a little too hard, "that it is a betrayal of the child to pass him without knowledge of the basics. You think repeating a grade is hard on him? How about life as an illiterate? How easy do you think that is?"

Instead of flak for this controversial policy, I received massive parental support. The parents were sick of excuses. They wanted and welcomed real education. My work on Carroll Street awakened a certain community pride and got many parents involved with the school. I set out to make that happen at Eastside.

One of the first things I did to reach out to the community was to formally introduce myself and my program at neighborhood churches. Each week I would attend a different service and, with the help of concerned ministers, would be given some minutes to address the congregation, among whom sat many an Eastside parent.

"The Sunday pulpit may seem to some an unusual place to find a high school administrator," I said to one such gathering.

"But I feel in my heart, and your pastor agrees with me, that the house of the Lord is indeed an appropriate place to address this very serious issue. Good people, I am here to speak to you on a matter that concerns nothing less than the salvation of your children's souls."

I acquainted them with myself and my beliefs, especially that it is through discipline and hard work that a person truly overcomes and achieves. I informed them of my two decades of educational experience: a teacher, the head of the superintendent's reading skills program, and a grammar school principal. I pointed to my success at PS 6, and I promised similar accomplishment at Eastside.

"Already I have made the building something to again be proud of, and have revamped my staff, expurgating all incompetents. Already I have made the yard, the corridors, and the classrooms safe from violence, extortions, molestations, and drugs, and I vow to you that they will remain safe. I ask you, I invite you all, to come out to the school and see the benign transformation taking shape. Please, do not lose faith in education. Do not simply turn your backs on Eastside because of its reprehensible past, but come and judge for yourselves. Come and get involved in your children's future. We at Eastside need your cooperation in order to carry my reforms to their best effect. I need you to give me the opportunity to extend to your children the opportunities a true education offers. These kids have been written off by many, but never by me. I will turn this school around and thus turn their lives around. I promise you I will give each youth the chance he or she deserves, and has so far been denied."

On one occasion, because the minister had graciously offered me as much time as I wished, and because the congregation was obviously quite receptive, I went more deeply into the subject of black people and education:

"In the 1920s, even in the Jim Crow South, there were a number of outstanding black high schools. St. Augustine High School and Xavier Prep in New Orleans, Booker T. Washington High School in Atlanta, Dunbar High School in Washington, D.C., Frederick Douglass High School in Baltimore, to name several of the most outstanding. These were segregated schools, before the Civil Rights Movement, before modern liberalism, after the Republican Party had ceased paying lip-service to the blacks and before the Democratic Party had commenced with their version of the same. These were schools supervised in the main by prejudiced and ofttimes openly hostile officials, schools for which the vast majority of the white majority did not give half a hoot any day of the week. They did not have fine facilities, nor small classes. They certainly did not have adequate financial means. What they did have, however, were discipline and learning. What they did have was academic achievement. From 1918 to 1923, Dunbar High School, for example, sent 25 students to Ivy League colleges, from which they graduated.

"I highly doubt there is an inner-city high school in the country today—in this modern, progressive, enlightened era full of festering sores—that can match Dunbar's erstwhile achievement. I know that Eastside cannot. I hope that through our efforts someday it will. Prudence, however, and honesty forbid me from speaking so optimistically about the pandemonic halls located in the killing fields of Detroit and the South Side of Chicago, or in the ganglands of L.A., or the wastelands of the Bronx, Camden, and Houston. There the college entrance rate is low, and declining. There the dropout and illiteracy rates are high, and climbing. There the family unit is broken down.

"Yes, there were hardships in the Old South. Yes, there was great injustice, great poverty, piercing sorrows, mind-mangling frustrations, shocking acts of cruelty, violence, and repression. Undeniably. But the black woman and black man and, consequently, the black child of that era did not, as they all too frequently do today, give up. They had heart, they had pertinacity. They found love and help, respect and renewal, from their close and inclusive families. And, as true family members, each returned these invigorating facets of support. Furthermore, these families made up church-going congregations, which spawned inspiring and purposeful preachers and leaders, who stimulated the minds and the souls, who reinforced the message implanted in early youth by parents and grandparents, older brothers and sisters, aunts and uncles, cousins and family friends: If you persist you will survive, if you work hard and do not give up, though the obstacles are many and the road is hard and long, you can advance, you can succeed, your life will have meaning, even joy.

"A high regard for education as the surest and most decent

way to advance grew from this communion of family and church.

"Then, in several waves, great masses of blacks came north, into the northern cities, seeking jobs. These people were, many of them, cut off from their roots—from their families, their churches, and their traditions. In the cities, the young blacks, especially the males, were led away by all the vices and addictions that plague us even more so today. The Civil Rights Movement of the 1950s and 1960s, which was led by educated blacks with strong ties to family and church, procured great gains for the black people, and for all people, most of all enshrining the concept of equal opportunity in federal law. But less than a year after the signing of the Civil Rights Act into law, Watts erupted, with Detroit, Baltimore, Newark, and other cities, soon following suit. Why? Because—let's face it—these dissolute and alienated urban blacks did not know how to combat the inequities harming them in a rational, organized, and nonviolent way. They were not even able to discern the victory Martin Luther King and the other Civil Rights Movement participants had already won. They simply blamed Whitey for all their troubles and let their hate and want drive them berserk. They were as much frustrated with themselves as with the system.

"The main results of the riots have been the proliferation of welfare, the quota system, and the dumbed-down education system for the inner cities. There has been an abominable marriage between those who rise to power by throwing money at the disadvantaged, and the foolish among the disadvantaged who prefer reliance on the dole to working to advance themselves. It is neo-paternalism, it is degrading, and it is rampant.

"Back in the 18th century, the Irish parliamentarian, Edmund Burke, referred to a 'species of benevolence, which arises from contempt.' Why, I wonder, why can't some people see that the limousine liberal who is tossing them a handout is often saying in his heart (and to his buddies) that these people are inferior, because they need the hand-out?

"This contemptuous and contemptible system tells the youth, 'You don't have to work in school: we'll pass you along, and we'll give you a diploma.' It tells the ignorant graduate, 'You don't have to be qualified for a job: we'll give you a job.' And to those who cannot even hold these jobs, or who are too busy selling and

VERNON REGIONAL
JUNIOR COLLEGE LIBRARY

doing dope to want a job, the system says 'Don't work: we'll give you welfare.' And it says to young girls, 'Go ahead, get pregnant: we'll pay for the baby.' In fact, they'll pay every time the foolish young girl gets pregnant, whether or not she's a good mother, or able to teach her children anything other than how to get on and stay on welfare.

"And still vice leads the people astray. Indeed, now more than ever. Drugs, weapons, prostitution, crime. Nor is it Whitey, for all the social and economic inequities yet extant, who forces a particular black or Hispanic to push the needle into the vein or pull the trigger. You cannot call all white people the descendants of slavemasters, or even legitimately blame the ones who are. And you cannot attribute all your difficulties to the fact that your ancestors were slaves. Don't you see how that is a copout, and an abnegation of your integrity? Don't you realize that such an attitude curtails your capacity to accomplish anything worthwhile? Great black leaders from various points on the political spectrum—Marcus Garvey, Booker T. Washington, Malcolm X—all of them denounced this terrible habit of self-degradation. Don't you know that there is such a thing as personal responsibility?

"Personal responsibility. But how often is there a home with two parents? The national average for single-parent households in the inner cities is between 50 and 60 percent. It is the same for Eastside: more than half the kids come from single-parent homes. And we all know that this parent is almost always the woman. The men are gone."—I paused, looked out over the congregation, about 80 percent of which was female, and let my words sink in—"The children have no fathers. The deleterious effect of this can be seen most readily in the wild and refractory behavior of our young males. Their poor mothers cannot control them, nor deter them from their mad race to addiction, and prison, and the early grave. Despite all the strength of character and determination daily exhibited by black women, until the men again become responsible human beings and work to restore the family unit, the inner-city black community will continue in peril, like a ship without a rudder.

"The hope, the only valid hope, is quality education. We must now strive for it without the help of many strong families. But strive we absolutely must. At Eastside, I see to it that education means more than just book learning. We are teaching youths to become responsible, accountable adults, good citizens, who will become the good parents, the mothers and the fathers of the future. That is why this hope is valid. Eastside is a starting point—as every school should be—for rebuilding an inner-city community. It is a battleground, where we are fighting the good fight. We need assistance, and you, parents, you are our natural allies. You must come and join in the fight. At stake is nothing less than the quality of the future."

I received an ovation for that speech. More importantly, a number of Eastside parents who were in the congregation, as well as a few people who did not have children attending, came out to the school to measure my words by the patent truth.

From the beginning of my reign, Eastside has been encouraging parental and community involvement in school programs and projects, like anti-drug seminars, Career Day, the different choirs and clubs, assemblies covering a wide variety of subjects, and all sorts of fundraisers. In tempering tough discipline with benevolence, I more than tripled the number of after-school clubs, increased and enlivened assemblies, and initiated numerous other extracurricular events, asking and receiving help from the community—from the parents and such organizations as the Lions and the Elks.

I reorganized the Home School Council (what we used to call the PTA), subdividing it into five units: one for each grade level, and a full council for Hispanic parents. Hispanics, too, in coming north to the cities in search of employment, have been cut off from their roots and, in some respects, have been even more alienated than blacks because of the language barrier. One-third of the kids attending Eastside are Hispanic and two-thirds are black. So that the Hispanic parents' voices and particular concerns would not be lost in the voice of the majority, I had one council organized solely for Hispanics. Of course, all the councils interact and often coordinate activities.

The councils meet on a regular basis to discuss pertinent issues. Not only parents and teachers are involved—students and administrators are invited as well. The parents, however, run the show. Each council elects officers from among the parents, and all the officers form an Executive Council that also has regular meetings, usually to coordinate fundraising.

Teachers and administrators attend to keep the parents informed of what's happening at the school, and abreast of any changes, like new federal legislation or new state guidelines. The parents, naturally, bring up matters of concern to them and their kids, like drug counseling and AIDS awareness, or improving the library's stock, or school facilities for the handicapped. There is a special interest among the parents of the juniors and seniors to learn all they can about the possibilities of financial aid for college and other post-high-school training. The Guidance Department regularly sends representatives to the councils armed with such information.

Importantly, parents get to meet each other. Those with particular problems have found support and friendship from other, empathetic adults who have survived similar difficulties, and something of that old, good, family-based neighborhood spirit lives again. And the parents get to know the school. When parents first started coming out—as almost no one had in the former administration—they saw the immaculate state of classroom and corridor, the utter absence of damage and graffiti, the works of art and various other amenities of the new Eastside High. They also received first-hand experience of the reality of my no-exceptions pass and ID system. Involved and impressed parents interested yet others in our reborn institution. This still goes on, with a growing number of parents finding time to participate. One mother so clearly perceived the value of our labor of love that she left her day-job and took in sewing at night, in order to volunteer on a regular basis at the school.

That woman radiated love and effort. She possessed vision, dedication, nobility of soul. But would she have come forward if a competent, energetic principal had not arrived upon the scene and begun to transform pandemonium into sanity? No, intelligent people do not lend their time to lost causes.

The Home School Councils, through concerned parents, keep the school in touch with numerous civic and business organizations, many of which are intent on real community improvement, and have come to recognize Eastside as the horse to hitch their wagons to. The churches also have stayed involved. The councils place notices on the churches' bulletin boards, and many of the pastors make announcements concerning the Home School Councils, and Eastside in general, from their pulpits. The ministers themselves have been strong allies.

Pastor Frederick LaGarde of Paterson's Community Baptist Church of Love, the church to which I belong and am a trustee, has over the years been one of the staunchest allies of the new Eastside, and of education in general. Furthemore, he is a shining light in the community and a man I dearly love. We share the belief that church, school, and community must work together to resuscitate the inner city and rescue the future.

"One of the eternal verities, taught not only by Christianity, but by all true religions and philosophies," says Pastor LaGarde, who was one of Martin Luther King, Jr.'s, lieutenants during the Civil Rights struggle, "is that you reap but what you sow. Principal Clark has sown order and benevolence, has worked his field with energy and care, and has reaped an abundant harvest that is a sign of hope for us all. He appealed to and gained the support of a significant number of parents, as he turned a blackboard jungle into a citadel of education."

Which caused, by the way, Dr. Stephen Ferraro, to lose a lot of business. He is the general practitioner whose office is near Eastside High. It was to Dr. Ferraro that the bulk of serious cuts, traumas, contusions, concussions, and broken bones occurring at Eastside (B.C.) were taken. He did not lack for work. Since the autumn of 1982, however, Dr. Ferraro has estimated that his business from the high school is down 90 percent. He doesn't mind; he is pleased that violence has so greatly diminished at the former trouble spot. Dr. Ferraro does not hesitate to give the credit for this successful operation to "Doctor" Joe Clark.

Parents quickly learned of the fulfillment of my promise from my most consistent and effective envoys—their children. It is by these scales that a principal is most significantly judged. Homes were abuzz with what was happening at Eastside:

- "Mr. Clark challenged the drug-dealers, said they'd get hurt if they came around!"
- "Mr. Clark is everywhere, no outsiders get in anymore!"
- "He had the cops lead some guy away in handcuffs!"
- "Kids are getting instantly suspended for fighting or cutting class, and if he catches you smoking reefer he'll throw you out! He means it!"

Declarations very much like these were excitedly made in hundreds of living rooms and kitchens, to hundreds of impressed and relieved parents. I know because Eastside parents told us.

In addition, many adults saw what they had not seen for a generation—kids with homework, every night. Some were even drawn into helping their offspring, as it should be. Parents also observed changes in their and their neighbors' youngsters' attitudes and behavior—being hoody or lethargic was on the way out, looking neat and being responsible were on the rise. We were making a difference. Even before the newspapers (with one exception) paid us any attention, we were the biggest news in town. When it became necessary to dismiss those 300 so-called students, I knew I could count on parental support. When that lone woman announced her intent to protest the action against her non-productive child, I knew I had only to call to gather a parental legion. I had reached them, touched them, and could galvanize them in a day.

I never start a war I cannot win.

But this war is not over. Attendance is certainly up at the Home School Councils. Parental and all-around community involvement with the school has markedly increased. Yet, though scores of adults are active in supporting Eastside, hundreds of others are still seldom, or never, heard from. But there are their children, every day before my eyes, the odds against them increased by the folly of parental apathy. I will not increase the folly through apathy on my part.

One morning, about three years ago, a female Hispanic student complained to one of her teachers that her father was beating her. The teacher at once informed the department head who immediately contacted Mrs. Maus, the executive vice principal. Mrs. Maus, knowing my directive that such cases be addressed without delay, paged me over the loudspeaker. Ten minutes later I was closeted with the student. Before another ten minutes went by I was asking one of the teachers who serve as Eastside's liaisons to the Hispanic community to come and translate: not because I could not understand her imperfect English, but because I could not understand it perfectly. In cases like these, clarity is everything.

"He beat me!" she said, through the translator. "He slapped me across the face, and he hit me again and again with his fists, on my arms and my sides. Do you want to see the marks?"

"That won't be necessary, Maria." It was obvious that she was very upset. Indeed, she was furious. It burns me up to hear about the physical abuse of a defenseless person. But I reminded myself to proceed gingerly. She might have been exaggerating the matter, or blaming the father for what someone else had done. I turned to the liaison. "Mr. Martinez, as soon as we are finished here, you will accompany Maria to the social services office and have the nurse examine her. First, however, I want to learn why her father did such a thing."

"He hates me!" she cried, and glared at the wall.

"Now, child," I said, "I doubt your father hates you."

"*Es verdad*, Mr. Clark! He doesn't want me to have any fun. He never lets me go anywhere. And now, now when I find a boyfriend I love, he beats me up for seeing him!" Her eyes were blazing. "He is a beast, a monster!" She raised a clenched, trembling fist. "I want to kill him!"

I let some time go by, to give the young woman a chance to calm down, then had Martinez take her to the nurse. He wasn't long in getting back to me. Maria did indeed have black-and-blue marks on her body. "Do you want me to phone the father, Mr. Clark?" he asked.

"No, Mr. Martinez, that is something I should do. But it would be good if you were on another line, just in case he doesn't understand me. In fact, come right back to the main office. Leave Maria with Mrs. Maus. I'll call the father at work. Let's try to get to the bottom of this before she has to go home again."

The father received the news with proper gravity and promised to see me at the school the following day. Maria made plans to spend the night at her aunt's.

The next morning the three of us gathered at one end of the long table in the conference room. I had Mr. Martinez tell the father of the entire matter before us, short of telling him that if municipal and state agencies were brought into this affair he might, if he were indeed guilty of the abuse, lose custody of the girl. I wanted to give him the chance to tell his side of the story without frightening or seeming to threaten him. As it was, his nervousness, behind his stiff formal manner, was evident. His brow darkened, worry filled his eyes.

He avoided our eyes for some moments. When he did look at

me he maintained, for a few seconds, his formal posture. Then he trembled, broke, and began to weep.

"Yes, I struck her," he said. "I guess I lost control of myself and hit her too hard and too often. I feel terrible about it. But she infuriated me. She doesn't obey. I am her father, I love her, I try to discipline her for her own good. I didn't mean to hurt her. I meant to help her, to save her! You, you are Joe Clark. You know that children must be disciplined."

I asked: "What were you trying to save your daughter from?"

His eyes hardened. "From that bastard she has been seeing behind my back. Seeing, and God only knows what else! He's ten years older than Maria. It isn't love. He's just out for what he can get. I'm trying to save her from ending up pregnant, from ending up an unwed mother, ruining her life before she's really lived."

It gave me a moment's pause. Here was a man, a father, who had gone too far in his discipline, yet it was a decent end he was trying to achieve, and one with which I heartily agreed. Finally I said, "I understand your parental concern and I sympathize with your dilemma. I think, however, that your means are self-defeating. Losing your temper and hurting your daughter might well drive her away, into the arms of that older fellow, and into all the troubles you wish to prevent."

He pushed a hand through his hair and shook his head. "Mr. Clark, I very much fear that you are right." His voice was heavy with sorrow. He seemed again on the verge of tears. "Tell me then, what can I do?"

"I suggest, for starters, that you apologize to your daughter for losing your temper and being too harsh in punishment. You have told us that you love her. Perhaps you should tell her. Then explain your reasons for wanting her to be more careful. You must make a sincere effort to repair the relationship."

"Will you talk to her too, Mr. Clark? Will you tell her of the dangers?"

"I certainly will. You have my word. Also, sir, I would like it if you and your daughter were to speak with one of our guidance counselors. Maybe we can help you two understand each other. Do you agree to that?"

He nodded. "Si, Mr. Clark. If you think it is good I will try it."

Maria and her father had several sessions with our counselor, and a session with me as well. It soon came out that his apprehension for his daughter's safety was too extreme. He had been allowing her no social life whatsoever. We managed to convince him that our school dances and sports events were safe enough happenings, and Maria was granted permission to now and again come out and have fun. The affair with the older fellow soon evaporated, probably because it was based more on her rebelliousness than on anything else, and the causes of her rebellion were being addressed. Maria's father became active in the Hispanic Home School Council. Maria spent some time in the PASS program, joined some other clubs, and graduated two years ago. She's now a bilingual secretary.

Would that family's problem have been dealt with so expeditiously and effectively at Eastside B.C.? Only if Dr. Napier happened to be walking the corridors that day. Even then, though certainly something would have been done, I doubt the outcome would have proven so favorable, simply because a superintendent does not have unlimited time to do a principal's job for him. The case probably would have gone outside the school, very possibly to the detriment of all involved.

This principal, on the other hand, meets his job's managerial and ethical requirements. He knows that vigorous follow-through is essential. We did not look upon Maria's problem as solely a family matter and somehow divorced from the business of the school. Nor did we pass the buck to some social agency, though we certainly could have cried "child abuse" and done so, with little or no official reproach. Rather, we knew that the essence of education is the promotion of sanity and the protection from harm. We knew that the spirit of education is pro-life. To refuse to answer this girl's cry for help, and answer it well, would have been a dereliction of duty for an educator.

On another occasion a female student who came to me was distraught because of her father. He did not live with her and her mother, but the daughter simply was not prepared to let him walk out of her life. She wanted him to care, to love, to do right by her, to do his fatherly duty. This teenage girl's plea deeply moved me. I sought out the father, going to his ramshackle apartment. He wasn't at home, so I left a note: "Urgent, important, come see Principal Clark at once." He came, anxiously wanting to know what the problem was. "You are the problem!" I said, and lit into him with a full verbal attack. Shortly, his hard exterior cracked. He broke down and admitted he had been derelict and vowed to reach out to his daughter and help her. He has, apparently, kept his vow.

There have also been times when, having recognized a problem with a student and hit a dead end in seeking out a parent, I've appealed to an older brother or sister. I remember confronting one Hispanic man, an older brother of two of our students. I went to the garage where he worked, because the single mother would have nothing to do with me. He said it was none of his business, that he had worries enough, and he remained cold and unreceptive all the while I remonstrated. Two weeks later, however, he showed up at the school, wanting to know how his siblings were doing.

These are a few of the success stories, proofs that constantly reaching out on an individual basis can, and does, make a difference. Every student must have someone he or she can turn to, at least one door must always be open. Eastside, under Joe Clark, will always provide what help it can for the needy student, even when—nay, especially when—the parent is unresponsive.

Eastside has become the home a lot of these kids never had. Just recently, for example, I saw fit to remove the couches I had installed in the corridors in that first year. I had put them there to provide comfortable stopping places, where kids might chat or read a book in a warm and homelike atmosphere. But the couches had to come out, because kids were not going home. The kids were staying in the corridors long after the final bell, sitting on the couches, talking, reading, and doing homework.

I honestly wish they could stay longer if they so desired, but the school cannot provide the services necessary. I tell them to join an after-school club, where there are adult monitors. But I cannot turn the corridors into a living room, at least not yet.

The love of a few thousand kids can be a very tiring commodity. Sometimes, I simply go home and straight to bed—the tireless Joe Clark so damned tired, from having his arms tugged a hundred times each, filled to surfeit with all the dreams and worries, adventures and problems, of these affection-hungry youths. I lie in bed and my mind cries, "Parents, where are you? Fathers, where are you? Your children need you. They have me, but they need you too."

Insight E
THREE VERY SPECIAL YOUNG PEOPLE
•

As a parent I have always tried to fulfill the duties I, as a principal, expect of any parent. I have been, and am, deeply involved in the education of my three children.

When Joetta, now 26, and Joe, Jr., now 24, were pre-teens I enthusiastically encouraged their interest in track, not only because I myself had run cross country in college, but also because I knew that, under my guidance, their traveling around the country to compete in various track events would also serve as a series of learning opportunities. I never failed to take them to the museums, aquariums, and national monuments of the area we were visiting. They resented it a little at the time. They appreciate it now.

Joetta has gone on to become an international track star. She holds the world record in the 1,000 yard indoor event, as well as four American records. In 1988 she was the national 800-meter champion, and has won that race four times at the Vitalis/Meadowlands Invitational Meet. Also in 1988 Joetta went to Seoul, Korea, to compete in the Olympic Games, and was a semi-finalist in the 800. She is a graduate of the University of Tennessee with degrees in journalism and public relations, and is currently studying for her masters in the field of recreation. She is a sports consultant, a spokesperson for Nike, and a member of the State Attorney General's anti-drug division.

"I have had a hard time, at times, listening to the negative comments about my father," says Joetta. "I see him come home so tired from a long day's work, then hear some media people say that he was doing all this just for fun. But he's been that way for such a long time, long before he got any publicity. He's always been a strict disciplinarian who emphasizes the value of education and the old-fashioned work ethic. If he never got any publicity he'd still be doing things the same way. He even turned down a job with the Reagan administration to continue doing things his way at Eastside."

"My father has given each of us a tremendous amount of support," says Joe, Jr., who is a graduate of Villanova and is now studying for his masters in physical therapy. "The self-discipline I learned from his strict discipline helped me make it through college. I was traveling around to track and field events, and there were always so many social events happening, that if I didn't have the self-control to stay at the books I would really have hurt myself."

Joe, Jr., is a miler, who is considering a try-out for the 1992 Olympic Games.

My youngest child, Hazel, is 11 and attends South Orange Middle School. It makes me proud that she loves school so much. When you ask her what her favorite subject is, she says, "Social Studies, Gym, Art, Math, and English."

"Oh yes!" says Hazel, who wants someday to become a lawyer, "My father makes sure I do my homework. Sometimes he makes sure I do it even when I don't have any."

"He's a very caring man," says Joetta. "His concern as a father is that his kids will be able to take care of themselves."

8

TO REACH THE HEART
AND TURN IT

I KNEW when I took the Eastside job that if I was going to be a good principal—and I was going to be—I would have to be a surrogate father, too. A surrogate father with a few thousand kids. You hear some administrators complaining about it. More often you hear the thunderous silence of principals dodging the role. Every principalship has some degree of parental surrogacy built-in, but in an inner-city school it is a major part of the job. For many of these kids, Eastside is their only real chance at a decent life. If a youngster is blowing that chance I have to try to set him or her straight, in any valid way I can. And I have to be there when they reach out for me. A father doesn't let his kids go down.

One Saturday morning in early spring a few years ago, I was at Eastside, as I normally am on Saturdays, doing paperwork. Quiet, very few people about. Saturday is one of the few days I am in the office for longer than a several-minute interval. I was bending over some papers, pen in hand, when there was a knock on the door and one of the security guards escorted a young woman, one of our students, into the room.

"I have a problem, Mr. Clark."

I dismissed the guard and instructed the young woman, a 16-year-old, to take a seat. I recognized her and could have made a fairly accurate guess as to what the trouble was. But because she had come to me to talk, I let her do so.

"I'm sick of everything," she said. "I really am. Of my parents, of school, of living. Especially of living. It's all so hard, and crazy, and seems so pointless. I want to die, Mr. Clark. I really want to kill myself."

This was not the first time this student (I'll call her Shirley) had expressed that negative and pitiable desire. She had been confronted by one of her more perceptive teachers earlier in the school year, and thus was referred to a special unit of our Guidance Department called Choose Life. It was a program I had set up in direct response to a bizarre and disconcerting rash of teen suicides that had swept through New Jersey in the early 1980s, themselves a part of a grisly nationwide plague that still goes on. Choose Life had helped a number of confused and depressed youngsters, and seemed to have been helping Shirley. But, obviously, not enough.

I looked across the desk at this troubled girl and said to myself that the high-sounding platitudes and conventional theories had not yet cut it with her, and I'd be a class-A fool to suppose they would now, simply because I was repeating them. The best-intentioned words in the world can be empty noise at times like these. Yet she had come to me and was reaching out for help, real help, the kind she figured Joe Clark could deliver. So, Joe Clark was not going to let her down.

"Come with me!" I said in an authoritarian tone, leading Shirley out of the office. Along the empty corridor we marched, saying nothing. We mounted the stairs, to the second floor, to the third floor and, as she gave me an inquisitive glance, we climbed the final flight, pushed open a heavy door, and stepped out onto the roof.

"Over here!" I commanded, striding to the edge. There were mountainous, snowy-white clouds floating impassively above the shoddy buildings of "the poor side of town," Shirley's world. On the sidewalk across the street I spied a wino staggering pathetically along. Some youths in a thunderously loud car roared past. I looked down the sheer wall of the building, about a

40 foot drop to concrete and macadam. Shirley had stepped, hesitantly, timidly, to my side. "Look down!" I said. "Come on now, girl, look down!"

Finally, noticeably trembling, she leaned forward and gazed down. I stepped a little away from her. "Go ahead, Shirley," I said. "Jump! You're sick of living, you want out, you want to end it all. Here's your chance. I won't stop you. Splat on that hard ground and cancel your miserable existence. Go on, jump!"

I was lying of course. I'd not moved but a step or two away and was ready and quite able to yank her back if she made the least move toward self-destruction. But I felt supreme confidence that she would not. Indeed, she stood frozen there for a few seconds, having a sort of revelation, I suppose, that death is a lot less romantic when you're forced to look it in its grim face, when a good part of your life-loving being suddenly wakes from its torpor and shouts that the escape is not worth the price.

"What's the matter, girl? Why don't you jump? I thought you wanted to end it all."

She jumped all right. Back from the edge. Then backpeddled to about the center of the roof. "Oh no, Mr. Clark, I don't want to jump! I don't want to die!"

"But life is so tough, Shirley. You told me so yourself."

She was shaking her head, clutching her sides, and almost shouting. "But I don't want to die, Mr. Clark! I want to live!"

"Even though life is tough?"

"Yes sir! I want to live!"

"Because life is tough, Shirley."

"I know, I know. But it's all right. I want to live. I'm going to live."

Shirley went on to finish that school year and, a few years later, to graduate. She is still alive.

Alone, back in my office on that same afternoon, it occurred to me that this incident with Shirley was symbolic of a larger problem. Almost all of the kids in the inner city are suicidal. Not consciously, not overtly. But their bent and their habits, by the time they get to high school, are self-destructive. For most of them this is their last chance to turn around before facing the real world. At Eastside, I am their last chance, and I, by various means, take them to the edge, show them the sheer, pitiless drop, and challenge them to choose life.

The building at Eastside in 1982. (Courtesy Ed Hill, *The Record*)

Here I am in the halls of P.S. 6, where I was principal before I came to Eastside. (Courtesy Ed Hill, *The Record*)

The neighborhood surrounding Eastside. (Courtesy Ed Hill, *The Record*)

Turning graffiti into art. (Courtesy Carmine Galasso, *The Record*)

Patrolling the grounds at Eastside, on the lookout for miscreants. (Courtesy Rich Gigli, *The Record*)

It is important to know the students personally and to take an interest in their lives—something all too many parents neglect. (Courtesy UPI/ Bettmann Newsphotos)

The immaculate hallways of Eastside provide an atmosphere where learning can take place. Note also how the students are unpretentiously yet tastefully attired. They are serious, in a businesslike way, about education—not about fashion trends. (Courtesy Ed Hill, *The Record*)

The support I have received from parents and students has been one of the most rewarding aspects of my time at Eastside. Here I am leading a rally in the school auditorium. (Courtesy UPI/Bettmann Newsphotos)

Athletics are important as long as they are kept in the proper perspective. They provide an outlet for healthy competition, help build school spirit (which I think is very important), and, especially for inner-city students, show that hard work can pay off in victory. (Courtesy Ed Hill, *The Record*)

I listen while Secretary of Education William J. Bennett holds forth in a classroom at Eastside. (Courtesy Carmine Galasso, *The Record*)

On the *Donahue* show exhorting parents to care about education and their children's futures. (Courtesy UPI/Bettmann Newsphotos)

At the premier of the film *Lean on Me.* I hope the success of the film will translate into more principals taking on the task of reforming their schools. (Courtesy Thomas Franklin, *North Jersey Newspapers*)

One young man, Lester, had been a problem to his mother for several years before becoming a freshman at Eastside. It was a situation we have seen far too often: A single, working mother who cannot control her young son. He was hanging out on the streets to the wee hours when only in the seventh grade, making money now and again by scouting and carrying for the drug pushers. Though he had undoubtedly tried some drugs, Lester was not an addict or a criminal. Not yet. In fact, he was an intelligent and fun-loving lad who could be quite likeable. But by the age of 13 he was almost a full-time wiseguy on his way to real arrogance and total disrespect of authority, and probably to a lot worse.

I spotted him the first day. Lester had heard about me. He was being extra careful in my presence, and extra polite. But he was transparent. The insolence and mischief were so evident in young Lester's face that I made a point of turning my back on him in such a way that I caught his reflection in the glass of a classroom door. Sure enough, Lester the wiseguy was aping me, showing off for his friends.

A few days later I spied him in the corridor, took him aside and gave him a mini-lecture. "Education is serious business," I said. "And it is a blessing. You are a fool if you blow your chance. Furthermore, Mr. Clown, if I learn of your behavior taking time away from the education of your schoolmates, you'll be out of here in a flash, and forced to find work with the circus!"

He seemed to take me seriously, but once again I detected a hidden, sneering attitude. There will be some trouble from this one, I said to myself.

About three weeks later one of my teachers asked to see me. Lester, who had been doing nothing but clowning in her freshman English class, had that day called her a racist. This was an elderly, capable white woman, who had been teaching for more than 30 years, and had stuck it out at Eastside through all the bad and chaotic times when, with her seniority and credentials, she could have transferred to any school in the system. I knew her well. She was as much a racist as Sarah Vaughn. Nonetheless, in order to be as fair as possible, I corroborated her story by speaking with several of the students.

Lester had been fooling around as usual, trying to impress a girl. The teacher demanded his attention. He made a snide remark and continued with his foolishness. So the teacher took the tack of talking down to him, hoping to embarrass him into silence, if not enlightenment. That's what triggered the outbreak.

"Oh, little Lester, do you want some attention?" she said. "Is my little boy cranky?"

The other students giggled. But Lester, shamed and angry, shot right back. "You can't call me 'boy.' That's a racist remark. You're a racist, you're a racist!"

Having gotten the whole story I phoned the youth's mother. Surprise. She had been a student of mine at PS 6. She was abashed, and disconcerted. "I'll speak with him, of course," she said. "I'll punish him as well. But, honestly, I don't know what good it will do."

His mother spoke with him first. She upbraided him for wasting his education, for hanging out with drug users, for bringing shame on her and their family. I know for a fact that our talk inspired her to give Lester a lecture the likes of which he had never before experienced. And she called him wicked for making false and injurious accusations. That upbraiding did more good, I think, than she ever imagined.

Next I had at him. "Lester!" I boomed over the bullhorn. He stopped at the far end of the corridor, as the students filed into their classrooms. "Report to my office!"

I made him wait—ten minutes, fifteen minutes. I wanted him tense and frightened. Why not make him sweat? Were not his nascent racism and self-destruction much more frightening prospects? Finally I let him in and, as he was sitting down, I rose, fixing him, looming over him.

"Tell me, Lester," I said sternly. "Tell me what a racist is."

He lowered his eyes, started to mumble. "Speak up!" I shouted. "What is a racist?"

"Someone who hates black people," he blurted.

"Wrong! A racist is someone whose words and actions are destructive to a particular race, any race. Do you understand that?"

"Yes, sir," he muttered.

I paced around a bit, let it sink in. "And what, Lester," I asked some 30 seconds later, "is a black dope addict?"

"A black dope addict?"

"You heard me! A black dope addict. A junkie, a coke-head, a crack addict! I'm sure you have seen such people, haven't you?"

"Aaa, yes. Yes, Mr. Clark." He was puzzled. His eyes following me.

"Then tell me!" I boomed.

"A black dope addict. A black dope addict is a, a black person who's hooked on dope."

"Yes. But what else is he, or she?"

"What else? He's a . . . a. . . ." He fell silent and stared at me.

I leaned over, got right in his face, and said it in a low, firm voice.

"A black dope addict, Lester, is a racist!" I pulled back, shouted. "Yes, a racist! Because his actions are destructive to a particular race. His own! The black dope addicts are destroying themselves and bringing shame, degradation, and ill-will upon their people. They are racists, real racists. And if you become like one of them, you'll be a racist too!"

I returned to my desk. Lester was motionless, still staring. "That's all," I said. "Return to class." He walked out like a zombie.

About two weeks after this confrontation I heard from the English teacher. Lester was a changed student. He had asked to be assigned a special book report in order to make up for the disruptions he'd caused. And he had done the report well.

"Why shouldn't he have?" I replied to her astonished look. "He's an intelligent young man."

It is not, of course, all drama and confrontations at Eastside, though it is an exciting place and I do my best to keep things lively. These kids have to deal with one or more aspects of inner-city hell every day. I make certain that the school they attend is not one of them. One of my instruments in this ongoing endeavor is the loudspeaker. I get on it every morning and exhort students to give 100 percent to gain the most possible from this day's education. I say:

"You are here to learn so that you can achieve something in your lives. You were not meant to be drains on society, but contributors. It is to your great advantage to make use of these hours of free instruction. Don't let yourselves down. Don't let Eastside down. With self-discipline and hard work you can overcome the obstacles blocking your paths to achievement. It is up to you. Be responsible."

I also congratulate Lisa for the improvement in her math grades, or Ronnie for scoring his first varsity basket, or Keith and Reva and Francisca for the lovely pictures they've drawn for the corridor, or Susan and Rose for their beautiful rendition of the alma mater. There is always, each day, something to commend someone for, and I make sure I know what it is before classes begin. Some of these youngsters have never been commended for anything at all since the day they were born. Their spirits have been buried under the inner-city avalanche, but a little attention, a little love, can bring on a smiling resurrection. And Lisa and Ronnie and Rose, not feeling so down now, can wake up to the opportunities, right there before their eyes, for making happiness a real part of their futures. Self-hate and depression do no one any good, and they must be combated or they become habitual.

In addition, I occasionally hand out little gifts to students, girls mostly, who might not have achieved anything special of late, but who I feel are neglected and could use a morale booster. Nothing much: teddybears, baskets of fruit, corsages. Out of my own pocket, of course. They are often the girls who are not considered good-looking, the ones the boys ignore. And why should they suffer or get down on themselves because of the caprices of birth? The gifts, like the commendations, do pick up spirits, and increase the chances for actual learning taking place.

On the other hand, if something deplorable has occurred that concerns the school's image, and therefore the student-body, I announce it. We face up to it together.

"One of our students, I won't say the name," I once declared over the loudspeaker, "was, yesterday after school, apprehended in the act of shoplifting. This fills me with sorrow and brings shame upon our excellent institution. Imagine what sort of ammunition this solitary incident gives those small and bigoted minds that think lowly of us, that would rather see Eastside fail and return to the ignominious way it was than admit our accomplishment is real. Now, because of one thief, they will say we are a den of thieves. I implore you, students, from the bottom of my heart, do not bring disgrace upon our school. Conduct your lives after school with the dignity you display while you are here.

"As for shoplifting, the thief robs the material object, but he also robs his own soul of its integrity. I will not tolerate thieves. Decent people work for and earn their goods, just like decent students work for and earn their education. If you lack decency you don't belong in this school."

At the end of first period, a profound sense of sorrow and shame pervaded the corridors. I saw it in the students' faces, heard it in their words with me. And I shared in this sense of disappointment and shame. Yet, even then I began to cheer up, because these faces signaled that my message, my dual message on dishonor and theft, had gotten through.

I cannot claim to know the names of all the students in the school. Just most of them. And, through faces as well as surnames, I recognize the younger brothers and sisters of current or former students. I introduce myself, make them feel welcome. There truly is a warm feeling among us. We are a prime example of the real extended family.

Most of the school day I am in the corridors. I read the youngsters' faces as they pass, discerning playfulness, endeavor, nobility of soul, as well as the full gamut of troubles. Moreover, there is always a constant, lively patter among these marvelous youths, something that I easily join in with. I learn all the news. Kids are always telling you—by body language, by what they say, by what they don't say—what's going on at school, at home, among this and that clique. Always telling you, provided they trust you and you know how to listen. The ersatz principal who stays cooped up in the office, who is seldom accessible, seldom mingling in the halls, how can he or she possibly be tuned into this wonderful, inexhaustible source of information? And how can he be a consistently effective administrator when he is out of touch with the students?

A young male, one afternoon, was obviously feeling low. I knew he was struggling in a few classes, but I had also heard that he wanted to buy a car and was complaining that his after-school job provided nowhere near enough money.

"Money troubles?" I said, after throwing an arm around him and drawing him aside.

A principal who simply asks how a youngster is doing in class runs the risk of sounding like an automaton, thereby receiving an automatic, and empty, reply. It is much better to sound like a mind reader.

His eyebrows went up a bit, then he nodded his head. "Yeah, Mr. Clark. Never got enough."

"Flipping burgers at McDonald's just doesn't pay enough, does it?"

He was impressed. The principal cared enough to know where he worked. But once again his face fell back into depression. "No, Mr. Clark, it doesn't."

"So what are you going to do about it?"

We walked slowly along for a number of steps before he replied. "I'm gonna drop out and get a real job."

"Come with me." Once again to my office, because that's where I keep my Louisville Slugger. Once we were inside I handed him the bat. "Nice one, eh? You play ball?"

"Yeah," he said. "A little."

"Then you are quite aware that it's three strikes you're out?"

"Sure, Mr. Clark. Who doesn't know that?"

"Did you know this? You are black, a member of a minority." I shot one finger into the air. "That's strike one! You are poor." Two fingers up. "Steee-rike two! It's you're turn at bat, son. Your first time at the plate, and it might be your last time too, because if you strike out you'll get sent right back down. Understand me?"

"Yeah, but it ain't fair. I gotta come up with two strikes against me!"

"You're right. It isn't fair. But there's nothing you can do about that. You're up there and you've got one cut. That's a strike-throwing pitcher on the mound, believe me, so you've got to swing and you've got to make it count. If you drop out of school, that's strike three. You're out of the batter's box, out of the ball game, and off the team. You're finished."

He stood there a moment, the bat resting on his shoulder. Then he brought it down, placed it gently back in its corner. "I know you mean well, Mr. Clark," he said. "But that three-strike thing, that's just a story. I gotta make some real money, and a real job's the way to do it."

There's another benefit of being an energetic and accessible principal, a benefit with which, I believe, all truly active people are to some degree familiar. I mean the way different things, coming from different corners, seem to fall so neatly together at certain times. It's more than mere luck, because it stems from persistent labor. It's more like a justly deserved bonus.

"Just a story, eh?" I said, opening the top drawer of my desk. "A real job, you say." I searched a little, then took out a xeroxed sheet that had accompanied a letter I'd received from a concerned businessman in Trenton who had heard me speak. It was an article from *Black Enterprise* magazine and contained some very significant figures, which this businessman had underlined. I knew right away that this sheet would come in handy, and sooner than later. "Let me tell you how serious that third strike is."

I read an underlined section. "Between 1970 and 1984 New York City lost 492,000 jobs previously filled by high school dropouts, and gained some 239,000 requiring some college." I repeated the figures, and quoted similar ones concerning Philadelphia. I explained them, made sure he understood just what they meant. "This is a trend. There are fewer and fewer jobs every year for unskilled laborers, for dropouts. Forty, fifty years ago, a dropout could get work on a farm. No more. Fifteen, twenty years back he might find a factory or construction job that paid enough to raise him out of poverty. It can't be done today. Face it. The factory jobs have gone overseas." I explained about the relocation of corporate factories and the cheaper labor market in the Far East. "There are still jobs in the U.S., a lot of jobs right here in New Jersey, but they are for people who know how to read and write, people who can work word processors and other computer equipment, people who can communicate clearly and intelligently. Businesses are so desperate for people with basic office skills that many companies are running their own reading and math classes. Think. Would they spend the money to do that if they weren't desperately in need? The jobs are there, good-paying jobs too. But you have to be prepared in order to get hired. Right here, at Eastside, is where you get that preparation."

He was listening now. I know because his questions made me say just about everything over again. He pressed me for detail after detail. What businesses were hiring? How much do office workers make? Could you go right from high school to working a computer?

I loved the questions. They're the sort of questions I want every one of my students to ask, and ask until they get the answers. "We have computer studies right here!" I boomed. "Don't you pay any attention at all? You know what your problem is? Impatience. You're like the fool who ran down to the river to build a raft, but forgot to bring an axe to chop the wood. You want a new car, so you're about to throw away your best chance and jump right on out to grab a job that isn't there. You're having trouble with your English class, so you get impatient and want to forget about it. But if you took the time to learn your English, and earn your diploma, you could get the job that would permit you to buy the car."

By the time I was through haranguing that young man, I had not only convinced him to stay in school, but also to sign up for one of our after-school tutorial classes in reading. When he claimed that the extra class would interfere with his hours at McDonald's, I said, "You tell your manager exactly why you need your hours changed, and I guarantee that he'll work out a new schedule for you. If he refuses, I will go down there and see that he does!"

The manager understood and agreed to change his schedule. Would I have confronted him if he had not? Damn right I would have. And I would have found another part-time job for my student if it had come to that. I might be theatrical, but I am no sham.

Our near-dropout, by the way, now plans a career in computers. This young man would most certainly have left school (and would, almost as certainly, have ruined his life) if I, his principal, were not in close, constant, affectionate, and perceptive contact with the student-body.

Eastside, since I've been at the helm, has had a vibrant, ongoing campaign to keep kids in school. My own persistent messages are bolstered by an accessible guidance staff, numerous posters in the halls, and guest speakers. Nor is it just posters and programs, for they would be dead letters without the active, caring people behind them. We drive the message home. In the year before I arrived (1981-82) 736 students dropped out of Eastside and into the inner-city abyss. Last year fewer than 200 dropped out.

It is, with these youths, a question of direction. It is a question of priorities. So many of them lack discipline at home. Here we give them discipline, certain and unswerving. They like it. They know that we respect their lives enough to try to help. I'm confident that the great majority of young people in school situations where orderliness is lacking would welcome discipline if someone would only re-institute it.

We also make further amends for the deterioration of their home-life by being genuinely affectionate. Through this "tough love" they gain a new perspective on the role and value of authority. So we are able to work effectively against the jumbled and false priorities with which the ruined homes, the street, and the floundering grammar schools have infected them. The lies and vices of the street are the enemy. At Eastside I give the enemy no quarter.

One of my innovations was the Virgins' Club, a support-group for young women to, basically, allow them to make up their own minds about their respective futures. Libertines, of course, scoffed. They suggested that family planning classes were the way to go. But family planning courses around the country don't seem to have slowed down the alarming rate of inner-city teen pregnancies at all. We needed something inspirational, something to give the old virtues a chance to fight against modern libertinism. The scoffers do not seem to understand how, on the street, the pressures on a teenage girl to "give it up" are constant, intense, and often utterly devoid of affection.

"I was always being made to think that I had to have sex in order to be cool, to be one of the gang," a senior who belonged to the club told me a day or two before graduation. She and her girlfriend had come in early to show me a poster they had made for the next year's freshmen: "Babies Making Babies Doesn't Make Sense," it said, over a drawing of a big infant holding a smaller one, who was holding a yet tinier baby. They'd also come to thank me for, among other things, starting the Virgins' Club.

"I was uncertain," the first one went on, after they had gotten over some giggles and bashful glances. "My mother used to warn me about boys, but I saw that she did what she pleased. Oh there were a couple times I almost did it. Once the guy got so mad I thought he might use his knife on me! But Connie got me to join the club, and it really helped. After hearing some of the girls' stories, I started to finally realize that those boys just wanted to use me for their fun. And if one of them got me pregnant, he would have disappeared, just like my cousin Loretta's so-called boyfriend did."

"Plus you never know when you could have gotten AIDS," said Connie, quite correctly.

That's another thing the scoffers seem to have forgotten. I was not only battling against teen pregnancy, but also against AIDS, which is more rampant in the inner cities of the East Coast than anywhere else in the nation. Junkies carry it, prostitutes carry it. How easy, really, for some wild young male to contract the fatal disease and transmit it to some naive girl who felt she had to have sex to be cool and accepted. The Virgins' Club addressed the AIDS issue as well. It liberated young women from intimidation, kept them informed, raised their awareness.

"Now when we decide to give it up," said Connie with a smile, "we won't be catching any disease."

"And only getting pregnant if we want to!" added her equally jocular friend.

"You young ladies are very wise," was all I could manage to say.

Things were, by no means, always so pleasant. One student broke into tears the moment I shut the office door.

"I'm pregnant, Mr. Clark!" she stammered. "I'm four months pregnant!"

I led her to a seat and handed her some tissues. "Clara, do your parents know?"

"No one knows. Only the people at the clinic."

"How about the young man?"

"Young man? How about goddamn bastard! I don't want him to know. I'd rather shoot him than tell him!" She cried some more. I sat silently, waiting for her to calm down a little. "I . . . I need your help, Mr. Clark," she said at last.

"What can I do for you?"

"You've helped a lotta people before, Mr. Clark. You gave Freddy money to buy some shoes, and you gave Cecilia the bus-fare to visit her sister in Pennsylvania, and you. . . ."

"Clara, what do you want?"

She hung her head. "I need some money, Mr. Clark. For an abortion."

I stared at her, this 15-year-old who, before this afternoon, had always appeared so happy and innocent. An abortion. I did not know what to say, but had to say something. "Clara, dry your eyes. Compose yourself. I want you to go to your next class, then come back to see me."

"Are you going to help me, Mr. Clark?"

"I want to help you, Clara." I led her to the door. "I need some time to think the whole thing through. Come back after class."

Usually, as I've said, I am in the office for only short periods of time: a brief meeting, a phone call. On this day I gave do-not-disturb instructions, locked the door, and sat at my desk for an hour, mostly with my head in my hands.

An abortion. I pondered the dilemma. Clara was a fairly good student, a good young woman. And she was fortunate enough to have parents who were still together. An abortion? No, as a Christian I could not countenance it. My heart went out to her, but I simply could not finance her move. I had been born into much harder circumstances than this child would be. No, let the child be born into the challenge of life, and enrich all life by meeting the challenge.

Clara returned hopeful, and my words brought the tears again. But she did listen as I explained myself and offered advice.

"I will inform your parents, if you wish me to. And if you decide to have the child but cannot keep it, I will help you place it somewhere until you are ready."

"But Mr. Clark, the whole school is going to find out!" she cried, on the verge of another burst of tears.

"No one, Clara, is going to find out. I promise you. We'll find a solution for you. We'll arrange for a tutor to come out to your home."

"But, but. . . ." More tears. And my own welling in my eyes. I put my arms around her.

"Child, it isn't easy, but, if you take my advice, you can make it through."

"Will you call my mother, Mr. Clark?"

"Whenever you wish."

Clara had the baby, a boy. She, in concert with her parents, arranged for an aunt and uncle to care for the infant while Clara finished school. Clara is still at Eastside, getting good grades, and some vocational training in tailoring to help prepare her for the future.

I also had to grapple with the proposal for a day care center at the school. Surely it is a good idea to free up young mothers to obtain their educations and diplomas. But after days of running the argument back and forth in my mind, I decided against it. To have a day care facility at Eastside would, in our environment, encourage female students to risk pregnancy. Some, I fear, might even fall into that slovenly welfare habit of having babies just to get checks. My goal is to have people climb out of that hole, to be responsible citizens who will resurrect the true family ethic. No, Eastside's message must be: Do not become pregnant while in high school. It is too heavy a burden to take on without proper forethought. Get an education. Then think about what you want to do with your life. Don't let a few minutes of passion rob you of your future.

Sending the right message, always that is the mission. It is at the root of education. Nonetheless, the message does not always get through.

There was one young man who had an exceptional mind, but he had been running with an extremely wild crowd since he was 7 or 8. He behaved himself at school, because he knew I would not tolerate hooliganism. But it was evident that he was using drugs and probably staying out much of the night. His grades, which could have been A's, always hovered around low C. I tried many times, and in different ways, to pull him off the road to destruction. I upbraided him, I mocked him, I spoke frankly with him—all to no avail. Early on he had developed a way of dealing with people in authority: always easy, even gracious in manner, as if he agreed with you entirely, but the mind was always shut tight.

He even graduated. But as I handed him the diploma I looked in his eyes and knew he was lost. Eastside was his last chance, and we had lost him. I had lost him.

He is in prison now, for robbery and manslaughter. He never communicates with me. But his sister does. She too graduated from Eastside, and she knows I tried to help her brother. Last Christmas she sent me a letter, which included a newspaper clipping. It was a list compiled by the Reverend C. Galea who worked with young lawbreakers, and asked them to draw up a code for their parents.

This code contained sound advice for adults, such as: keep your temper, don't get strung out on booze or pills, be strict, stay on that pedestal, tell us God is not dead, get tough, punish us when we need it, call our bluffs, be honest, and praise us when we deserve it. My young correspondent, Jimmy's sister, wrote:

"These are things my and Jimmy's parents should have practiced. You were these things for us, Mr. Clark. But our parents weren't, and that's why Jimmy already hated the world too much by the time he came to Eastside, and why he's in prison today. It makes me feel a little better that kids in prison drew up this code. Maybe Jimmy too will finally begin to see the light."

It brought some consolation to me—and a confirmation of my belief—to read that kids really want to be treated in a fair and disciplined way. It brought some heartache too. She had underlined "booze or pills." Their parents were addicts.

To say that the United States faces a drug problem is an understatement on a par with saying that France faced a problem of German immigration in 1940. Drugs are a deadly plague, assaulting our nation everywhere. The attack is particularly evil upon the children and the schools of our inner cities. Nevertheless, I have driven drug sales and drug use, all of it, out of Eastside High. But I do not delude myself that the drug monster is defeated. I keep constant vigil. And keep the anti-drug message pumping.

One morning a student felt it necessary to inform me that another student was hiding drugs in his locker. I do not encourage informants—I don't think squealing is a very good character trait. But when you are inspiring people you must live with the overzealous.

"All right," I said to the informant, "tell me which locker it is."

He did so. I waited until the period ended, wanting the corridors filled with students. Then I began my march, bullhorn in hand. "Drugs?" I boomed as I strode, turning everyone's head. "Is it possible that there are still drugs in our dear Eastside?" Students stopped dead in their tracks or turned and followed me. "There will be a slight delay in the commencement of the next period," I declared, to make sure of a large audience, "until I determine if that plague called drugs is trying once again to infect us!"

I halted before the locker. The corridor, now packed solid to either side, began to buzz with the whispered name of the locker's user. "Silence!" I declared. "I will have no prejudgments or slanderous remarks. In this nation a person is innocent until proven guilty." Then, with an anxious silence prevailing, I did not, as expected, command the student to come forth and open his locker. Rather, I made a request of the hall monitor.

"Mr. Conklin, would you please open the fire-emergency closet and procure me the axe."

What a murmur those words initiated. Eyes went wide, jaws dropped. The crowd parted for Mr. Conklin like the Red Sea and he came through bearing that long-hafted axe as though it were some ritualistic weapon. Ceremoniously, I handed my bullhorn to another teacher and received the impressive tool. I deliberately spent some moments looking it over, feeling its heft. It was a valuable image I was implanting and I saw no reason not to be thorough.

"Everyone, stand back!"

They gave me plenty of room. I shouldered the axe, set my feet, raised it high, and came down with the heavy blade—bang!—on the door handle of the locker. A large dent, the metal bolt still holding. Again I set myself. The atmosphere was electric. Again the axe cut the air, banged the locker door, caving it in, loosening the bolt. One more time, swoosh and crash. And another. And a fifth. The door, now a wreck, popped feebly open.

My audience, I assure you, was impressed. They were flabbergasted. I searched the almost empty locker, then turned and, prominently holding the axe before my chest, addressed everyone.

"No drugs here. My information was mistaken. But my purpose was absolutely right and my determination remains unswerving and indefatigable. Drugs will never be tolerated here. Not for an instant." My face was fierce, my eyes blazing with righteousness, as I scanned the youthful faces in the crowd. I felt satisfied that the plan had succeeded. These youths would, for the rest of their lives, carry with them the vivid and shocking image of a man in a three-piece suit, a man of position and authority, their high school principal, wielding a powerful axe, and striking vigorously and repeatedly against not just a locker door, no, but against the evil monster itself, Drugs.

"All right," I said, relaxing my pose, "return to class. Don't dally."

When the axe was put back and the corridor was again empty, I had the young man whose locker was now destroyed brought to me. "I apologize," I said, "for bringing any suspicion upon you."

"That's okay, Mr. Clark," he said, glancing past me at the banged-up, hanging door, obviously still astonished by the event.

"Here's a hall pass. Take your things and see Mrs. Reed. She'll assign you a new locker."

"Yes, Mr. Clark."

"Oh, and Lawrence," I added, once he was standing next to the demolished door. He turned. "If, by chance, you are using any drugs, stop. They will kill you."

I left Lawrence to ponder death and, a few hours later, caught up with the erring informer. I ushered him into an empty classroom, locked the door, and lambasted him for squealing, then for spreading falsehood.

"But I only wanted to help, Mr. Clark," the poor guy finally blubbered. "I only wanted to help!"

"To help, is it? That's all you wanted to do?" I could have shredded him then. I mean, there was more than a little chance that, in addition to crusading zeal, some amount of envy and vendetta were fueling his motivation. This is not abstract speculation: I knew the boy. I could have dissected his soul before his eyes and given him a greater reason for tears. But I controlled myself. It was unnecessary. No example for a principal to set. Instead I used the opportunity to turn the lecture back to education.

"Just wanting to help isn't helping. You have to know how to help. Otherwise you just mess things up. If you want to help a mechanic but don't know anything about car engines, if you try to help you'll only make matters worse. When you get married and have kids, if you just want to raise a decent family, but you don't have the education to land a decent job, then you're only going to hurt your wife and kids and make yourself miserable. Stop trying to help me; help yourself while you still have the chance. Stop spying on people and get the education you come here for. Learn something, make something of yourself. Only then will you be able to really help anyone else."

I turned and headed for the door. He started to follow. "No, you sit here another 15 minutes and think about what I've said."

You have to reach their hearts and turn them around. They have energy, they have intelligence, they have courage. All of which will go to waste if that inner-city mindset is not broken.

In the spring of 1983—still my first school year as principal—some concerned parents and I spearheaded a drive to institute a dress code, which centered on the introduction of uniforms, at Eastside. We knew this would be a struggle—all worthwhile reform always is. On an April evening, before a large audience of parents in the school's auditorium, I stepped to the podium and fired the opening salvo.

"It is obvious," I said, "that far too many students pay much more attention to fashions—to what each and the other has on—than to learning. Anyone who knows the situation here knows I am not at all exaggerating. They compete with each other regarding clothes and appearance, but not regarding academic achievement, where competition can be healthy. They work long hours at their part-time jobs solely to afford fancy outfits to show off in school. But they have no homework to show because they had no time to do it. Hundreds upon hundreds of black and Hispanic youths look forward to nothing so much as Prom night, so they can deck themselves in silks and jewels and ride in a limousine with a white chauffeur. Such expensive and wrongheaded fantasies! Such attitudes to carry into adult life! Parents, your children's priorities are topsy-turvy! They have Calvin Klein jeans on their behinds and nothing in their minds!"

That line brought applause and laughter. Many more parents added their support, several claiming that the expense of outfitting their fashion-crazed kids for school was more than they could bear. But there was opposition as well, cries against regimentation and the curtailment of freedom of choice, as well as accusations that we were trying to ape the parochial schools, (which, I suppose, means that I was being accused of popery). Well, I drew up a report and tried to make the matter crystal clear. After all, what good is freedom of choice to an uneducated, unemployable dandy or doll? At any rate, I presented my report to the Board of Education.

"Principal Clark," said the chairman, "we request that you hold in abeyance your efforts to implement a dress code for Eastside High until a committee studies the question in more depth."

I acceded. A parents' committee was formed, studied the question, and opted for voluntary uniforms. They then found a merchant who promised to make outfits available at a set price in return for the committee's guarantee to buy a certain number. All seemed to be going well. Then the owner of a department store in downtown Paterson, learned that the Eastside parents' committee was about to do lucrative business with a store in nearby Elmwood Park, the store that supplies uniforms to Paterson Catholic. The merchant phoned the committee.

"Why didn't you tell me you were looking?" he said to one of the co-presidents. "I'm a merchant in your own town!"

"Because," the woman replied, "we understood that you had stopped making uniforms."

He had, but he was willing to start up again. "Let me show you some samples," he said.

"Okay. We're having a meeting tomorrow night. Come and show us."

He complained that it was on too short notice and that he was busy re-doing his store. The merchant wanted a promise that the parents wouldn't buy until they'd seen his proposal. The co-president said the committee could extend no such promise. The next evening the local store owner did not attend the meeting, but the proprietor of the Elmwood Park store did, and the parents' committee agreed to buy his product.

The Paterson merchant exploded. "Paterson stores are going to lose $400,000 in business this year," he said on the phone and in the papers, "because all the Eastside High families will be shopping in Elmwood Park. Once they're there they won't buy only uniforms, but coats, shoes, handbags, all sorts of items!"

He did have a point, though all downtown merchants did not agree. But then he began making wild accusations against the Board of Education, against Superintendent Napier, against the parents' committee, and against me.

September had come along. Many Eastside pupils were wearing the new uniforms. I took the opportunity, now that the uniform matter seemed to have been settled, to help the trend along and instituted (by way of prohibiting hindrances to the educational process) a modified dress code. Which is to say I banned jeans, miniskirts, and profusions of jewelry. The merchant, already hot, saw me taking yet more business away from him, and lashed out.

"He's forcing them into uniforms by forbidding the things students wear to school," he roared. "I would like to stop this nonsense. I think it's outrageous."

I was ready to fire back. I was going to do so the very next day. Frank Napier must have read my mind, because he phoned me at home.

"Listen, I don't want you getting embroiled with this store owner," he said.

"But he's accusing all of us of some sort of conspiracy. He doesn't care a tinker's damn about education. I want to announce my purpose: to get the kids' minds off fashions and on to lessons."

"Joe, announce your purpose in some other way, in any way you like. Just don't go responding to him. Don't mention him. If the reporters ask you, tell 'em I gagged you."

"But. . . !"

"Listen. I'm the boss. I hired you. I share your purpose. But I don't want the schools wrangling with the downtown merchants. It makes it harder for me to get along with City Hall. So can it."

I did. The merchant turned his wrath on Napier. He would not accept that it had been the independent decision of the Eastside parents, that no school system contract was involved. He wouldn't quit. He organized other merchants, and they put pressure on City Hall, which leaned on the Board of Education, which let the parents know that maybe the uniforms were not such a good idea.

"Politics," I shrugged and said to a member of the parents' committee who asked me what was going on.

"It's bad," she said. "Looks like we're not going to be ordering any more uniforms."

"I'll be candid with you." We had gone outside the school for privacy, standing on a side-door landing. "I would fight this thing tooth and nail if I thought there was the slightest chance of winning. There just isn't. If I went after the merchant or the board, it would result in bumping heads with Frank Napier, who is Eastside's dear friend and ardent supporter. That would be senseless and suicidal. Discretion tells me to walk away."

"That means we all walk away," she said quite listlessly. "We've lost."

"Wait a minute, Emma, wait a minute! We may have lost the battle, but we are going to win the war."

"How's that?"

"My dress code. That's staying."

The ban against jeans, miniskirts, all those gold chains, and any outlandish costumery—that's in place to this day. The superintendent backed me on it. The other powers that be backed off as the uniforms disappeared. My staff and I enforce it assiduously. And we are, over the years, winning the war. Most of Eastside's students understand that to look sharp you need not fuss and flash and promenade all day long. They dress neatly, like their teachers and administrators, in a range between conservative and acceptably casual. A businesslike atmosphere, one in which to take education seriously, prevails. The extravagance of outfit, the competitive fashion show—these have been diminished greatly.

I remember when some people from *Time* magazine were out at the school, asking me questions, taking pictures. I was giving them the tour and, as we turned a corridor corner, we came upon a young woman who was wearing a quite alluring blouse. It was white and gauzy, unmistakably see-through. She smiled at us. "Good morning, Mr. Clark."

"Good morning, Francine." I surmised that she didn't think she was breaking any rules. After all, there was no formal regulation stating "no transparent clothes." "Francine darling," I said, putting my arm around her, and having her walk along with us, "you look pretty as usual. In fact, my dear, you look too pretty in that gauzy blouse. Francine, how can we expect any of the boys to be able to concentrate on their schoolwork while you are strutting around in that captivating blouse? Impossible. Grades are just going to plummet. I'll be forced to close the whole school before the first lunch period. Just because of your very pretty, of your too pretty, blouse. Now, Francine, you wouldn't want me to have to close down dear old Eastside, would you?"

She was blushing, but not overmuch. "Oh no, Mr. Clark. It's my favorite place."

"Mine too, my dear. So, in order to save dear old Eastside High from a fatal case of ga-ga minds, I think, Francine, that you should, right this minute, go to the office, procure a pass, then go home and change your blouse. Will you do that, darling?"

She was smiling cheerfully, as were the people from *Time*. "Certainly, Mr. Clark. No problem."

Off she went, and we went on with the tour. About an hour later, as I was seeing my visitors to the main door, up comes little Francine, even more bright and cheerful, wearing a stylish, blue, opaque blouse. "How's this, Mr. Clark?" she asked.

"That is superb, Francine," I said. "It does not lessen your prettiness one iota. And now the rest of the school might get some learning done."

She walked off smiling. She told that story for days, and eventually, I'm sure, the real message got through to her. I reach them any way I can. By playfulness or a fire-axe. By a precipitous drop or a teddybear. Francine, Connie, Lester, Shirley, and all the others. Thinking of Shirley again, thinking of standing there at the edge ready to grab her if need be, I am reminded of the young man I did have to physically hold back from destruction.

It was after a football game, across town at Hinchcliffe Stadium. This lad, Roger, was one of our linemen. He'd played his heart out, but we had lost the game by two points. Some of the students from the winning school got rowdy and loud-mouthed after their victory. I made sure to position myself near their buses, to prevent any confrontations. The police had the same thought in mind; a half dozen of them, young and tense, were milling near the gate area.

Up comes Roger, alone and disgruntled. "Hey, Refrigerator," hollered one of the out-of-towners from a bus window. Roger was a large young man. "Your mama oughta keep you out of the icebox!"

Roger didn't say anything. He just turned and headed for the out-of-towners' bus, intent, I imagine, on scrapping with the whole load of them. Three policemen—no frail fellows among them either—blocked his way. I was hurrying over. The bus pulled off, and a few loudmouths took the opportunity to hurl some further epithets at infuriated Roger. Unable to reach his antagonists, Roger unwisely took his frustration out on the police. He stood there defiantly when they told him to move on, calling them vile names, and even, just as I was running up, making threatening gestures.

The police were hollering back now. "I said get moving!" shouted one.

"You deaf, fella?" screamed another.

"Go to hell, cop!" said Roger.

The three officers, hands on billy clubs, moved forward. Roger stood his ground. They were inches away from painful contact and all the unfortunate ramifications, when I, with no time to talk, flung my arms around big Roger's big waist and, with more strength than I ever knew I possessed, spun him around and out of the path of the police. The two of us went stumbling to one side and tumbled to the ground. Roger turned bellowing, about to belt his assailant. Then saw it was me, sprawled on my butt next to him, and at once stopped his hand.

"Mr. Clark!"

"Roger, you fool!" I hollered, "You're disgracing us all. I ought to knock your teeth out!"

He went immediately from shock to shame and hung his head. "I'm sorry, Mr. Clark. I'm in a bad mood."

"You were almost in the hospital. And then in jail."

The police officers were standing over us. One of Eastside's coaches had somewhat calmed them down. I clambered to my feet. "I apologize for our student," I said.

"Long as everything's okay now," one officer replied.

"I can handle the situation, officer," I assured him.

One of the other policemen suddenly burst into laughter. "I'm sure you can, Joe Clark!" he cried, as the laughter and amusement spread among the other people who'd gathered around. "I'm sure you can!"

9

CRISIS

IN EVERY managerial job, just when you think you have everything under control, chaos reasserts itself.

In late October of 1984, my third year at Eastside's helm, on a Friday after classes, a fight erupted just outside the schoolyard gate, between two male students, a black and a Hispanic. I was standing in the outer office looking over a department report. A student burst in and shouted the news. I dropped the report and ran out of the building and across the back lawn.

The street was a crowd of youths, some of them not Eastside students, and some of these not so young. It took me a few seconds to spot the fight. Then I suddenly saw the two combatants in each other's grip, bumping off a parked car and falling together to the street.

"Now the young fools are going to kill each other!" I cried, prying my way through the crowd.

Closest to the fight were a score or more supporters, both male and female, for each participant. They were shoving and threatening one another, and hurling loud epithets—racial epithets. Seeing the glaring dichotomy between the groups, and hearing those harsh, barbaric insults, I was for one second stopped in my tracks, stung by the terrible feeling that a bloody race riot was about to erupt before my eyes. Indeed, just a few feet away another black-Hispanic fight had already begun.

I had entered this explosive inner circle just as the squad cars were arriving, causing much of the crowd to break up and flow along the street. Though I grabbed hold of one of the fighters, the police were not going to let me handle this one by myself. (In fact, I later received an admonition from the mayor for meddling outside my jurisdiction.) Yet I took note of many of the youths from either side of the altercation. Several of the black youths I recognized as novice members of a cult or gang that had been infiltrating our student body since the end of the previous school year. As the police were hustling the two combatants into a car, a black youth, from half a block away, shouted the gang's name.

"The Five Percenters cannot be defeated!"

"We are the gods!" hollered another, his fist in the air.

The Five Percenters, a radical offshoot of the Black Muslim faith, was begun by some dissidents in Harlem in the wild 1960s. For all I know, some of them might have done good things somewhere. But in the inner city of Paterson in the 1980s, under the direction of the deadbeat gurus who organized and incited them, they were an insidious contagion to the minds and souls of poor black youths seeking self-importance, adventure, and panaceas. They were a holier-than-thou bunch, the predestined five percent of black people, as they would have it, who were to lead some of their people (ten percent) out of modern-day bondage and unto salvation, while the majority of the black people, as well as everyone else on the planet, was damned.

I have great respect for the Muslim community. Islam teaches that you must work for what you desire, and that you do not drain the system, tenets with which I am in full agreement. Radical offshoots practicing bigotry and promising pie-in-the-sky are something else again. This was rabble rousing, fanaticism, egomania, and hatred, a new manifestation of the same disease that has always lurked among the world's dissatisfied. The Five Percenters were even so presumptuous as to call themselves gods (the males) and queens (the females), and to give themselves names like Justice, Power, Truth.

Since September I had noticed the hold this sect had on some students, and I had heard that some welfare-leech downtown was their pooh-bah. I was looking into the activities of this guy, and had spoken here and there to a number of students and parents about the cultish gang. Yet I had underestimated the group's influence at Eastside, and this violent black-Hispanic face-off, this sudden appearance of racism, took me totally by surprise.

Several students had received scrapes and bruises in the near melee, which had moved away from the interference of the authorities and continued. I detained some Hispanics and blacks who had gone, or almost gone, head to head.

"You a Five Percenter?" I asked, challenging a frowning black youth.

"No, Mr. Clark, I ain't."

"Then what the hell were you fighting for?"

" 'Cause Muhammed Truth said the latinos are killing blacks in Haiti, and that they're trying to take over this country, and change the language, and make the blacks slaves again like they do all the time in South America."

"And you believe that hogwash?" I hollered. "Muhammed Truth ought to change his name again, this time to Bonehead Lie. And he should change yours to Nitwit Follower." I paced around, controlling my exasperation. "I mean, why is it? Why is it you listen to a wiseguy punk and jump into a fight because he tells you the moon's made of green cheese, but you don't listen to your math teacher or your history teacher, people who really are telling you some truth and giving you a chance to make something out of your life? Why is that? Is it because the miscreant calls himself Truth? Well, listen to this. I'm changing my name too. My name is now Education. Education Clark. Follow me. I'm your ticket out!"

I went home that evening determined to begin a major in-school campaign against the noisome group. I had started to map out a strategy when I received a call. It was Mrs. Woods, one of our parent-volunteers.

"I thought you ought to know, Mr. Clark. It is a wild and shameful night in Paterson."

Numerous fights were breaking out in all sections of the city, fights between black and Hispanic youths. Mrs. Woods' husband had a police-band radio, and they were listening to the frequent calls: first this street, then that park, then that parking lot. It was an unpredictable, mobile rumble, baffling the police and terrifying the citizenry.

"And there are Five Percenters among them, Mr. Clark," she said. "Some of the ones who've been caught are calling themselves Five Percenters."

"Any of them our students?" I asked.

"I have no way of knowing just now," she said. "But, honestly, I would not be surprised."

"Nor would I, Mrs. Woods. But it's best not to leap to conclusions. If you learn any names, Mrs. Woods, or hear of any serious injuries, please don't hesitate to call."

No easy time sleeping that night, and small consolation that Mrs. Woods did not phone back. Staring up at the dark ceiling I would one moment tell myself, "At least there has been no bloodshed," only to think, the very next moment, "How do I know that? A kid could be bleeding to death in some garbage-strewn alley this very second!"

I went heartsick, as well, each time I thought about the effect of all this upon the school. Two years of order, peace, and academic improvement, and would it all be shot to hell because of this madness? No, no, I'd never allow that—I'd steer Eastside through this storm no matter what. But these street fights, especially along racial lines, were damaging our image by the hour. And it would be all the worse if someone got seriously hurt or if people got the idea that our high school was harboring some sort of racist or revolutionary gang.

And I pictured Dr. Napier bemoaning the failure to win an increase in the overall school budget, because politicians (feeding the fears and latent prejudices of the white majority) had beaten it down with a blown-up issue of "resurgent violence at Eastside High."

When I finally did doze off, a dream-image assailed me. It was the 1981 opening-day knifing, only more graphic, and with significant additions. In slow-motion the young black thug smiled maliciously and plunged the blade into the security guard's gut. Unnatural amounts of blood poured from the wound, as the guard drew a pistol and fired, not at his assailant, but at a young black girl who was simply standing in the corridor holding a teddybear I had given her. The bullet struck her in the head, and I awoke with a start from her heart-wrenching scream.

It was then I remembered that the security guard, the victim of the 1981 incident, had been Hispanic.

I had been prepared to combat and neutralize any bigotry at Eastside by or against whites. But I just hadn't viewed black-Hispanic hostility as a real threat. When learning of and later reviewing the 1981 knifing, I had seen it solely as a violent act against authority. Perhaps it was more than that. Perhaps it should have tipped me off. But then again, how could I have forseen incitement by pseudo-religious fanatics?

Nonetheless, the symbolism of the dream chilled me. Not at all a restful night. To be sure, being principal of Eastside High is a full-time job.

There was a report on the fights in the next day's paper. There had been several arrests, some adults, no one from Eastside. No one had been hospitalized. Yet, out at the school that Saturday I spoke with two parents and several guards and janitors who lived in the vicinity. They all agreed that the atmosphere was tense.

"I've heard some of that Five Percenter crap," a janitor told me. "They're saying that the latinos are Whitey's new slaves, that Whitey lets 'em into the country so they can take jobs away from the blacks."

We were standing just outside the rear entrance, looking at the scene of yesterday's chaos. Just across the street stood a jumbled row of 70- and 80-year-old houses, all in severe disrepair—the mark of the ghetto. "Harry," I said, "that certainly is crap." And just the sort of mental infection, I thought, to which the poor and uneducated are susceptible. I cannot end their poverty, not directly at any rate. But I can and will do battle against ignorance. "I'm going to run out the Five Percenters, Harry. There's going to be zero percent of them left at Eastside."

But even as I spoke, there were events taking shape that would make my task more difficult. Early that afternoon in the neighboring town of Montclair there was a high school football game between Montclair and Kennedy, which is Paterson's other, westside, high school. The two teams are traditional rivals and the rivalry is not always strictly wholesome or confined to the playing field. There is a disconcerting measure of animosity between the two municipalities, most noticeable among certain portions of the youth.

Montclair is far more affluent. Many kids come from stately houses set far back along wide, tree-shaded lanes. They drive the cars, wear the clothes, and have the plastic money and the cash that the poorer Paterson kids crave. Few Paterson kids have not seen a Montclair kid in a Mercedes or BMW buying dope on one of Paterson's more indigent streets. The student body of Kennedy is, on the whole, from economically better-off neighborhoods than the student body of Eastside, but it is still less (often much less) well off than the population of Montclair High. It aggravates the situation all the more that most Montclair kids are white, while Kennedy is a rainbow. And, of course, many Montclair youths are not above considering themselves divinely deserving simply by reason of their parents' or grandparents' toil, nor above propagating and practicing the crassest forms of prejudice. There is a history of feuds and mutual resentment.

That afternoon, while I pondered my problem and its possible solutions, Montclair beat Kennedy by a touchdown. There were some skirmishes during and after the game. There were also some Five Percenter propagandists at large, concentrating now on the disparity between whites and blacks.

The acrimony and the skirmishes carried over into a full-fledged rumble that night. The first confrontation was in the parking lot of a roller rink at a shopping mall in the nearby town of Wayne. There were about 200 youths from Paterson and Montclair. Paterson blacks and Hispanics were on the same side this time. The fool kids, hollering drunkenly, assaulted each other with bats and knives. There were a half dozen injuries, including a stabbing, and a dozen arrests.

The rumble broke up into numerous smaller fights in various hangouts in the area. A gang of Montclair youths, pumped to insanity pitch by drugs, booze, and brawling, pulled into a pizza parlor lot in Verona, spied four Hispanics in a pick-up truck, assumed they were from Paterson, and immediately attacked. They surrounded the vehicle and dragged out the amazed and terrified victims. A 19-year-old white youth tried to break up the fight. An affluent Montclair youth smashed this affluent Verona youth over the head with a golf club, knocking him into a coma. The four Hispanics were from Newark and had no idea why they had been assaulted. The Verona youth, Daniel O'Callaghan, died four days later.

Although, as far as anyone has been able to determine, none of the participants in this fatal rumble were Eastside students, I am relating the mad and tragic incident in some detail for several important reasons.

First, I believe it a clear indication that amorality, barbarity, and a disrespect for authority and civilization are by no means limited to inhabitants of the inner city, or members of a minority, or the "lower classes." This is an ongoing crisis that the whole nation must deal with, in the homes and in the schools. Secondly, the fights outside Eastside High on Friday and the resulting neighborhood tension, the news of the violence in Wayne and Verona, and the grisly report of a youth near death terrified a large portion of the Eastside community, as many people began to connect unconnected events and spread rumors. Chaos reasserts itself and can easily become a self-fulfilling prophecy if no one will challenge and quell it.

As soon as I learned on Sunday morning of this new violence, I factored in the panic-reaction on the part of parents, students, and teachers. I did not sit on my thumbs and vainly hope that the incidents in Wayne and Verona would have no impact upon Eastside. Rather, through Sunday, Monday, and Tuesday, I assiduously went after the facts. A principal simply cannot be disconnected from the community. I had to know the truth in order to tell the truth.

On Monday morning attendance at Eastside, normally around 90 percent, plummeted to less than half. The fearful parents kept their children home. These adults whose support I had won, through two years of earnest appeal and tireless work, were now in full retreat before the spectre of Eastside Past. I knew I had to act immediately, because if a fight did break out while the parents were unsupportive and the school was half empty, how would I regain their confidence, provided I was even permitted to try? And how could I properly discipline the wrongdoers if Napier, under pressure from an angry City Hall and an I-told-you-so board, were to waver in his support? What if then, with thugs on the rebound and certain students more brazen, another teacher were assaulted? The cries would quickly resound that Clark's luck had run out and that he was no better than the other principals. I am a confident man, but I am a realist too. I know the tables can turn, and swiftly. Looking out on the corridors and the faces of Eastside that Monday morning, I realized that all we had so far gained was suddenly in jeopardy.

One look outside the building at once confirmed my apprehension. As cockroaches scurry out of the woodwork when a room is dark, so did the thugs and assorted deviants, emboldened by the prospective triumph of darkness and disorder, crawl out of their haunts and mill menacingly around the gates of the school in surly clusters of five, eight, ten, and more.

"Bastards!" I muttered. "Leeches come to suck blood. But you won't get in. There won't be any FEAR STALKS EASTSIDE AGAIN headline. Even if the press comes gunning for me, they can walk the halls and see the transformation, they can talk to the kids and discover how much order and learning are now respected. No, this storm is not throwing me. This place is not reverting. I will burn you leeches off!"

The police, responding to the calls of various frightened citizens, had already scheduled extra patrols as well as plainclothes officers for the Eastside perimeter. I'd been told they were out there, but had yet to see them do anything. I called the police chief, and got a high-ranking officer.

"These thugs have to be removed before school is out," I said.

"But they don't appear to have done anything yet," he replied. "We're there, though, if something happens."

"If those miscreants are still there when school gets out, I guarantee you something will happen, something bad, and then it will be too late!" I knew what was going on: The police were content to wait it out, in hope that the day would pass without an incident. But I also knew that to be a foolhardy course, so I pressed my case. "I am lodging a complaint against them." I said. "They are a threat, they're loiterers, they're carrying weapons and dealing dope."

The police finally acted. They began ordering loiterers to move along and they spot-checked various characters. They made ten arrests that afternoon, for weapons possession, drugs, and failure to disperse. It was a great relief to see them in action. They were providing the sort of preventative measures the community needed and deeply desired. The thugs were gone by the time the students left for home. On Monday there were no fights.

In the meanwhile I set in motion my confrontation with the frightened parents.

"Mrs. McCabe," I said, "we must have the parents down here for a meeting. I must speak with them. Can we muster a telephone brigade?"

"I don't know how receptive they'll be, sir," she replied. "There's obviously a lot of fear. Who can say whether the ones we call will do their part and call others."

"We gain nothing by not trying. We'll just make more calls from here. Ask the teachers to volunteer. Ask them for me. Tell them I need their help, impress upon them that we are all in dire straits. I'll press staff members into service. We must get a large turnout."

"For when, Mr. Clark? Tonight?"

That notion gave me pause. I could have called the meeting for that very night. Hundreds of phones would ring, a hundred or more parents would come. A part of me wanted to say "Yes!" and round up these runaway parents as quickly as possible, get them back on my side before any other incidents made things worse. But I restrained myself. "No, Mrs. McCabe, tomorrow night." Urgency is one thing, panic another. An extra day would not only result in a larger audience, but would also be an extra day of proof that no incidents were going to endanger students and defile Eastside. "Tomorrow night at 8, in the auditorium."

The telephone work began at once. Mrs. McCabe and staff members solicited teachers to help out during their free periods, and almost all, perceptive of the danger, were willing. Capable students were asked to volunteer for their school and did so. Secretaries, file clerks, vice principals, and heads of departments were enlisted. Nor was this accelerated operation conducted in a haphazard fashion, which would assuredly have made a muddle, but telephone brigade procedure was already (because of my managerial innovations) in place, so that the lists of parents' names were headed by those adults who worked best and most responsibly with the school and who could best be relied upon to call other parents. Valuable time was saved. Every parent who had a phone was called. Of course some did not answer, but every phone rang.

As early as Monday afternoon we could make an informed guess that turnout would be good. In addition, I made an announcement that sent every student home with news of the meeting.

While my subordinates were getting the word out, I was busy on another front. First I suspended ten Five Percenter "queens" for improper garments disruptive to the educational atmosphere. They were wearing their turban-like headdresses. They complained, but left.

"My mama's going to call your superiors!" one young woman vowed.

"Tell your mama to please do," I retorted. "I will relish the opportunity of revealing to the whole city the doings of your ridiculous and malevolent cult!"

Then I located a black and a Hispanic who I had seen fighting each other in one of the Friday skirmishes, and met with each separately.

"Francisco," I said to the Hispanic student, pacing to and fro before him like a drill sergeant, "you really ought to be ashamed of yourself!"

"Why, Mr. Clark?" he bravely piped. "He provoked me. He mocked my family and my people."

"You are saying that he dishonored you?"

"Yes, Mr. Clark. He dishonored me."

"So you, in turn, dishonored your school."

"But I didn't mean to."

"But that doesn't matter, because you did dishonor your school. Your foolishness has made Eastside appear to the public as a hangout for brawlers and thugs." He was a good lad. I liked the way he stood straight-backed and took his lecture, although this did not cause me to ease up in the least. I shouted in his face. "That is why that police car is parked outside, as though this were some sort of prison, because the citizens of Paterson think Eastside has become a haven for hoodlums! You have dishonored your school. Furthermore, Francisco, it is you who have dishonored your family and your people."

His face flared. "But, Mr. Clark. . . !"

"Shut up and listen! You have given many people cause to think lowly of Hispanics, to think of them as brawlers and delinquents, as uneducable people. That is a disgrace and a dishonor to your family and your people. You ought to be ashamed."

He was ashamed, as well as angry and confused. He could not respond. I continued.

"Francisco, this is our school. This is our opportunity, yours and mine and the opportunity of everyone else who comes here, to prove to the world that just because people are poor or from a different culture, it does not mean that they cannot become decent, productive citizens. That's what Eastside is all about. But if we damage this school through dishonoring it, we'll eventually destroy it, and then we really will have nothing. Bring honor to your family and your people by honoring your school. It is the difference between civilization and barbarity. In the future, if you have trouble, any sort of trouble, come first to me. We'll get to the bottom of it together. We'll follow the law of civilization, not the law of the jungle. Do you understand me?"

"I think I do, Mr. Clark."

" 'Think' is a very good word. Think, Francisco, about what I've just said. And one thing more. I want your word that this fight is over and that there will be no others."

He gave it, and he promised to reason with any of his friends who seemed on the verge of breaking the peace. Through Francisco I extended my invitation to talk about problems. (In following months I got some takers.) Then I turned my attention to the other belligerent.

"So, Louis," I said, "I understand you have acquired a new religion."

"It's not something I can talk about, Mr. Clark," he replied.

"Very well." I paused a moment, then thundered. "Then maybe you can talk to me about that fight you were in on Friday afternoon, part of that idiotic brawl that has brought disgrace upon our school!"

"It wasn't my fault. He mocked my religion. Sometimes a man has got to fight."

"Oh, you are so right! You are absolutely correct! Sometimes a man must fight. Couldn't be more correct. Now tell me something, Louis." I was right in his face. "Am I a man?"

"Aaa, yes."

" 'Yes' who?"

"Yes, Mr. Clark."

"This isn't the street, Louis. This is a high school, an institute of learning. And I am the man, the man in charge here. And sometimes a man has to fight. And right now, this man before you is fighting because he has to, fighting for Eastside High." I thumped my chest. "You want a fight with this man, Louis?"

The tough guy was trembling a little then. "No, Mr. Clark, no sir. I got no quarrel with you."

"Oh yes you do, son! Yes, you damn well do. That's why I'm angry and in your face. You're hurting this school, and anyone who hurts this dear school has a helluva quarrel with me. You want a fight with me?"

He was scared now. He was thinking I might sock him where he stood. "No, Mr. Clark. No I don't."

"Then you don't fight in this school, near this school, or in this town or this state, or you will have a fight, I mean a fight like you have never known, with me! Am I making myself clear to you?"

"Yes, Mr. Clark."

"Are you going to be involved in any more fights with Francisco or anyone else?"

"No, Mr. Clark."

"All right then. Be a religious man and keep your word. If you have any quarrel with anyone, you come to me first and we'll work it out. Be straight with me, Louis, and I'll be straight with you. Keep in mind, I am also a religious man."

On Tuesday attendance was only a tad better. The thugs were again skulking along the fences. Again I pressed the police. They swept the school's perimeter and this time arrested twice as many people as they had the day before. In the building there was order, but tension also. I learned from a few students that the Five Percenters were after me.

"And what is it they're going to do to me, Andrew?"

He was standing with four or five other students, none of whom were smiling. "They said they're gonna kill you, Mr. Clark."

"Is that so? Well then, everybody will get a day or two off for the funeral. Now Louise, I don't want you backsliding in science when I'm gone."

I got a couple giggles. "But Mr. Clark," said Louise, "you're not going to let anyone kill you, are you?"

"I'm not going to die, darling, not for a long while. You see, I've just got too much hollering left in me, and God in His wisdom doesn't want me to waste all this good noise up in heaven where there's nobody to correct, so He's going to let me stay down here a while longer for hollering purposes." Finally I saw a few smiles light their faces. I felt better too, to realize once again that these young people cared for me. "Now you seekers of truth get along to class. And don't forget to remind your parents to come out tonight."

The phone brigade toiled on, as I went ahead with my investigation of the previous week's fights. I also made it a point to speak with other youths who had been in or close to Friday's action, working to turn them back from hate and vengeance. In the afternoon, passing through the office, I took a phone call.

"Clark, you're a dead man!" said a snarling, heavily aspirated voice. "You sacrileged the Prophet's people, and what happened to Malcolm X is going to happen to you!"

"And what's your Five Percenter name, punk?" I shot back. "Telephone Chicken?"

"I'm going to waste you, dictator."

"Why don't you come flying over right now, Telephone Chicken, and do that. You're a god, so fly on over and walk through the wall and waste me. Come on, Chicken, fly over. And I'll pluck your feathers and barbecue you!"

On Tuesday night more than 300 parents sat before me in the auditorium. The large turnout, I thought, might be a display of faith in Joe Clark and the new Eastside. Yet my optimism had to be restrained: At parent-school meetings throughout the nation, large turnouts almost always follow some act or threat of violence against the students. I could not presume that simply because the parents were there that they were on my side. Rather, I assumed the opposite, and addressed them to win them back.

The first order of business was to place the situation in proper perspective. I related a detailed account of the violence following the Saturday football game, quashing the rumors that anyone from Eastside was involved. "Let me remind you parents that adults have a duty, especially at times like these, to seek and sort out the facts, and to guard against being swept away by uninformed surmises and panicky speculations."

I then assured them of the safety of the student body, pointing not only to the last two days, but also to the last two years. "Remember? I came to you then and asked only for the chance to turn things around here. Is it not undeniably evident that I have delivered the goods? Have I not fulfilled my promise? Have I not run out the drug dealers and the hoodlums and made these halls safe? They are still safe. Do you think I would flag now?" I looked over that sea of faces and into pair after pair of attentive eyes. I shot my words like arrows, to strike their wavering hearts. "Do you suppose me a coward? Can you at all imagine that Joe Clark is going to lay down bullhorn and bat and hightail it because of one minor incident and the pusillanimous threats of lousy thugs? Listen to me. All Joe Clark lays down is the law at Eastside High. Fight, and you are suspended. That law stands. It will be enacted at once and without exceptions. And because students know this, now as much as ever, it never needs to be enacted. This school is not only safe, it's the safest place in Paterson."

I addressed the issue of the fight, explaining how I had met with the parties involved and had elicited a truce. I then blasted the Five Percenters.

"This principal is now at war with the Five Percenters cult. I refuse to have them contaminate Eastside's student body. I have been somewhat tolerant of them in the past, because I myself am a religious man and respect another's profession of faith. But I have come to the realization that this cult, as it exists in Paterson and at Eastside High, is not a religion at all, but a cesspool of hypocrisy and a front for hatred. Under the pretense of religion, they have been actively inciting racial confrontation between blacks and Hispanics. If that is not endangering education, then I don't know what is. Therefore, I will treat student Five Percenters as I do students carrying drugs. They will be suspended and, if they remain recalcitrant, they will be expelled!"

I contrasted the Five Percenters' high-minded credo with their scum-of-the-earth practices. Then I appealed directly to the parents.

"But this is not, and cannot be, my fight alone. You parents, you must speak to your children, you must share your time and knowledge with them. Tell them, explain so that they will understand, that these flimflam fix-all pseudo-religions and their conniving gurus are as numerous as flies around an outhouse, and worth a whole lot less. Tell them, as I tell them every day, that education is the only real solution, the only proven and genuine way out of poverty and its pain. I beseech you, parents, if you love your children, do not neglect this duty. Give them something real to believe in, or someone else, whose motives are less than love, will give them something shiny and false to follow.

"Teach your children how futile and self-destructive all forms of racism are. We blacks and Hispanics, the two most suffering and struggling minorities in the nation, we are brothers and sisters. To fight among ourselves is idiotic and suicidal. How can we afford it? How can we afford to let our children become slaves to prejudice and hate? Let's be realistic. We minorities have neither the time nor the opportunities to waste. We ought to be uniting for our mutual benefit, and uniting behind the things—like family and church and school—which truly are of lasting benefit. You people ought to know full well what hate can do. You ought not to have forgotten what a virulent plague it is. I beg of you to remember and transmit your knowledge, and to work assiduously to save your children from the plague of hate."

I paused. The fixed, concerned faces, as well as the lowered eyes, told me I had reached a great many. "You know me," I added. "You know that I will accomplish what I have promised. If ever I cannot you will have my resignation before you can ask. You know I have done and will do my job. Now, tonight, from the depths of my heart, I implore you, parents of Eastside, to do yours."

There was applause. It mattered little. What mattered greatly, and pleased my heart, was Wednesday's attendance. Back up to 90 percent, which is where it has stayed. The panic died down almost as quickly as it had flared up. There were no further incidents at Eastside. The police special patrol ceased on that Friday.

But I went on combating racism and fanaticism. I talked with every youngster who was at all connected with either side in that fight, preaching, in my Dirty Harry style, the gospel of reconciliation and brotherhood. It worked. That's one of the marvelous things about high school kids—you can still reach them. It is often very difficult, but it is not futile. A kid's life can be turned around in a day, in an hour, as long as someone is conscientiously working to create and capture those critical moments. I finally, for instance, got to speak with one of the Five Percenters about religion.

"What do you think about apartheid?" I asked.

"It's evil," he said.

"It most certainly is. But did you know that the Afrikaners believe they were chosen by God to enforce apartheid? Oh yes. They have their 'Covenant' to rule over all South Africa."

"But they're wrong."

"Absolutely wrong. So were the Nazis, but they too thought they were the chosen people. And the Moslem Arabs, what do you know about them?"

"That they worship Allah."

"They do. And they used to claim that Allah said it was okay for them to invade Africa and enslave black people. Did you know that?" He shook his head. "It's true. They took slaves out of Africa long before the white man, and they did it in the name of Allah."

He looked troubled. "I'd like to know more about this," he said.

I smiled, and sent him to the library.

The Paterson Five Percenter craze petered out soon after these events, and the ugly bigotry it had provoked returned to uneasy sleep.

10

A NECESSARY
PROVOCATION

I HAD A very important point to make on December 9, 1987, when I dismissed (permanently suspended) 25 sorry excuses for students. The next day, a Thursday, the Board of Education demanded that I re-instate them at once. The board's chairperson charged that "Principal Clark did not follow due process," and added that "the district guidelines say a principal in such cases must make a verbal and written effort to contact the parents concerned, as well as notify the Superintendent." Not only did I defy the board's directive, but that same day I permanently suspended another 41 so-called students.

"There is no way," I said, "that I am going to allow 75 or 100 non-learners to destroy the learning atmosphere for the other 3,000 students. Let alternative education settings be found for them."

The board fulminated. "He has until Monday at noon to let those students back in," their spokesperson stated, "or we will move to discipline him."

The media came out in force, several voices among them baying that Joe Clark had finally gone too far, and was now going to pay for his dictatorial methods. They tended to play up the story of my alleged insubordination. Quite early on in this crisis, which I had deliberately precipitated, the real and important issue was muddled and generally ignored.

Peter Tirri, the president of the Paterson Education Association (the local branch of the NEA) has been one of my most frequent and acerbic critics. Yet he clearly saw what the issue was and, on that same Thursday, clearly stated it.

"This board," said Tirri, "has absolutely ignored directives, calls, and requests for alternative education programs in this school district for six years. The cause of the problem is the board's failure to develop alternative programs. This is what forced Joe Clark into his decision."

That's precisely it. I knew that the dismissals would raise a big hullabaloo. But I was willing to risk disciplinary actions, even suspension, for the chance to publicly militate for an alternative program for both those over-aged underachievers and the disruptive students who are such a detriment to the education of the other students. Asking for such a program was, as Tirri pointed out, nothing new. But I thought that making use of what fame Eastside and I had accumulated over the last few years might prod excuse-rich beadledom to actually do something.

"I'm not saying such people can't be taught anything," I remarked to an anxious reporter who, I believe, was trying to put words in my mouth. "I'm making the point that we don't have the proper facilities to teach them here. I most certainly will not, for the cowardly motive of not rocking some bureaucratic boat, permit do-nothing students to slide through and receive a diploma they literally cannot read. Such students need to have, and should be allowed to acquire, useful skills, so they will have something to offer in their lifetimes. Bureaucrats and politicians put up fronts and play games, but this is not a cost-free situation. The district will either pay now, for an alternative program, or pay later, for jail space and welfare."

Another reporter wanted to view the records of those suspended. I told my executive vice-principal, Mrs. Maus, to make the papers available.

"Our system grants 5 credits for each course passed," she explained, while leading the young woman into her office. "One hundred and ten credits are needed to graduate." Then the sheets were laid out and the reporter saw:

- a 21-year-old student with 47 credits who, if permitted to continue along at that rate, might graduate by age 30;
- a 20-year-old student with 68 credits;
- a 20-year-old student with 65 credits;
- several 5-year students with around 50 credits;
- a few 4-year students with 30 credits, several more with 25, two with only 10, and one so-called student who was halfway through his fourth year at Eastside and had amassed a grand total of 5 credits, having by some miracle passed a freshman English class in his junior year with a low D.

The 66 so-called students totalled between them about 15 years of cuts, truancies, and suspension days.

These figures appeared in a local paper and Dr. Napier and I, among others, were quoted several times on the need for alternative education. But the focus of the local media coverage was on "heartless Joe Clark who put out those poor kids" and "renegade Joe Clark who won't heed his superiors."

On Friday, December 11, I answered the board's ultimatum by saying that I would permit 10 of the 66 to return, because these 10 had made earnest efforts to contact me and plead for one last chance to continue their education. The board members all knew me. They should have been able to decipher the conciliatory message within my statement, especially because Napier was serving as a sort of liaison between us. I was willing to help those students who were willing to make an effort to succeed, but I remained adamant that the board had to provide alternatives for youths who could do nothing in my classrooms but contaminate education.

The board had no desire, however, to compromise. Complete surrender to the bureaucratic will was demanded. "You must permit all the unduly expelled students to return by noon Monday," their spokesperson said. They thought they had me and were intent on teaching me who was boss.

They forgot that I am the more dedicated teacher.

That weekend I wrestled with the dilemma. I had to hold firm enough to make my point. But too much defiance would enflame passions all the more and would cause the issue to be lost in the ensuing dogfight. I had to find a middle course between a harmful surrender and useless obduracy, a way that would leave the door of compromise open. By Sunday evening I had settled on a course. Monday morning, I announced to the media battalions that I would comply with the Board of Education's order and re-admit the suspended students.

"But they will not be permitted back into classes," I added, even as some reporters were scribbling their 'Clark Backs Down' notations. "That would be an injustice to the other students. Rather, I will warehouse them in the auditorium until fitting alternative forms of schooling can be found for them."

So the reporters and the camera crews—after getting a few words and a few shots of the handful of youths who took advantage of the rescission and actually came back—hustled their equipment into their vans and rattled downtown to the board's office to hear what the chairperson thought of my latest move. Well, she didn't like it. She wanted unconditional surrender and, once again, rebuffed my attempt at compromise.

"Those students have rights," she said. "Each has a right to an education, which is something they will not receive sitting in the auditorium. The board insists that Principal Clark return those students to the normal course of the school day."

Such excellent, righteous words. The people's champion versus the heartless dictator. She of course made no mention of the other 3,000 students whose right to an education was being violated by 50 to 75 drags and disrupters, or of the right of a principal to ensure the best education for the greatest number of students.

The chairperson of the Board of Education avoided the issue—which was, I repeat, the need for alternative education programs—entirely. She got a lot of help from reporters who didn't know enough to ask her about it.

But several reporters did know enough to hurry around the block and huff up the stairs to the office of the superintendent of schools, to find out what he might have to say.

Dr. Napier wasted no words. "The problem is not Joe Clark. The problem is the lack of alternative education programs for chronic non-achievers. The board always pays lip service to proposals for such programs, but never puts its money where its mouth is."

Napier's words appeared in a few newspaper articles, but not on TV. That richer, fancier, and more frivolous medium must have reckoned that such talk was uninteresting and insignificant. Much better to show Clark and the board members snapping at each other, or let the audience see one of the non-achievers bending over an open text book, as if he had been doing that all along.

How true were the statements of the superintendent and Peter Tirri?

In 1975, a team-teaching program entitled Live & Learn was set up at Eastside, financed by federal CETA funds. The program not only taught basic skills to youngsters who had not been able to learn them in the classroom, it also involved municipal agencies and various businesses. Police officers, store managers, and others volunteered their time and tools (police report sheets, inventory lists, cash registers) and worked with Eastside teachers in showing the youths the practical value of math and literacy. Former non-achievers began to achieve, as well as to envision attainable futures for themselves. The program began with 40 students. By year's end 125 were enrolled. There was marked improvement, curiosity, enthusiasm, and community support. People around town were calling Live & Learn a success.

Then the national government redirected the CETA money. The Paterson Board of Education was petitioned and implored to pick up the tab and keep the program alive. The board refused. The program died. Live and learn.

In the notorious year of 1979, the State of New Jersey tried its hand at improving matters at Eastside by allocating funds for an ambitious, well-organized, and well-run alternative program called Pride in Eastside. Under proper supervision slow learners and non-learners were enlisted to repair and maintain their school, acquiring in the process basic academic skills and skills that prepared them for a number of jobs.

This program was, for its brief lifetime, so successful that it became the model for similar Pride programs throughout the nation. But the State's allocation ran out, and the Board of Education declined to provide another one. Pride in Eastside went the way of Live & Learn.

Yet again, in 1984, the Paterson Community Program, designed to teach academic and social skills, as well as to inspire self-esteem, through group counseling and work at hospitals and local businesses, moved along quite successfully for a number of months. But the original funding petered out and—you guessed it—the board turned its oligarchic back. End of program.

Those are the most promising of the programs that were allowed to die in infancy. There were others. Furthermore, a score or more of sound and interesting proposals in this vein made to the board over the years can be classified as stillborn. And all this despite the statistical evidence, which more than once has been placed before the eyes of the board, showing that in communities where alternative educational programs are in place in the high school the dropout rate has been no less than halved.

It is true that the voters and not the board members determine the size of the school budget. But the board makes policy and what was clearly the board's fault was its wrongheadedness on priorities. Alternative education in an inner city is a major priority. You will not find one administrator who toils in such a trying environment who does not agree, provided he or she is not too afraid to speak. But there is a pervasive cynicism among bureaucracies that all inner-city education is basically useless. Combine this prejudiced and disgusting attitude with nepotism, favoritism, in-fighting, and power of the purse, and you have a sure-fire prescription for inaction and the lip-service Napier condemned.

The superintendent called me as soon as the reporters had left his office and were rattling back across town to hound me and my students. He informed me of the board's unwillingness to meet me halfway.

"Frank, why in hell won't they be reasonable about this?"

"Because you've caught 'em with their pants down," he said. "For them to act rationally now, and to work with you for some sort of compromise solution, would bring to the fore all those years of their doing nothing. I mean, this is making the national news."

"But most of the board members are fairly new on the job. Why should they be embarrassed by what some other people did?"

"Hey Joe, is this brouhaha dulling your brain?" he said laughing. I stopped my pacing and leaned against the edge of the desk.

"Maybe so," I said.

Another laugh. "Well, you started it!"

Now I laughed as well. "That I did, Frank. That I did. But I didn't think they would be quite this pigheaded. Out with it now: what am I missing?"

"It's what we've talked about, Joe. It's about power. Even though the board has changed personnel, the present board doesn't want any negative stuff in the media. Because they're in a power struggle with me, Joe—or have you forgotten?—for control of the finances. If it gets across to enough people how they've laid down on the crucial issue of alternative ed, we might finally be able to end this dual control idiocy. So they want to keep the focus on what you are doing with those kids, and off what we're saying."

The system of dual control that gave the superintendent executive power, but handed the board the power of the purse, was the self-crippling system under which Paterson schools (until just recently) limped. Napier was saying "If you trust me with the job, trust me with the money needed to do the job. You can remove me if I don't do it well." I had, in the heat of the moment, forgotten this aspect, but remembered it in full before the superintendent was halfway finished with his reminder.

"The board's an anachronism," I said, glancing out the window at the ABC van pulling into a parking slot. "To set policy and hire and fire the superintendent, that should be the limit of their power. Let the Super control the purse totally, and rule over the principals without their damned interference. Those incompetents are threatening my job—me, the most competent administrator in the city! They won't let me run my own building."

"All true," said Napier. "What next?"

"Will they move to discipline me if I keep those kids in the auditorium?"

"Not sure. Probably."

"Let 'em. I'll compromise if they'll let me. I'll even let some of those kids return to classes, if I feel this experience has caused them to wake up and take their education seriously. But I know I cannot and will not allow most of them back."

"How's the atmosphere there," he asked.

"Excited. Excitable. Everybody is anxious over what might happen next."

He laughed again. "Me too."

I avoided the media people in the outer office and corridor, pausing only long enough to say, "Every visitor must sign in and must receive a pass. No exceptions."

I went to the auditorium, down to where the eight students were grouped. Eight here, ten already re-admitted to classes. That left 48, some portion of whom would undoubtedly show up on Tuesday. "I'm not here to promise you people anything," I said. "No one gets something for nothing in this life. Before last week you thought that was just one of Crazy Joe's sayings, didn't you, just something you giggled about when I said it over the loudspeaker. Now, perhaps, you are learning that it's the truth."

"But Mr. Clark," said one girl, "I've learned my lesson!"

"Have you, Doreen? Anyone else here who thinks he or she has learned their lesson?"

After a little hesitancy six of the remaining seven raised their hands. So I asked the solitary girl why she had not raised hers. "I don't know if I've learned my lesson yet, Mr. Clark," she said. "I just know I'm afraid right now."

"Don't let yourself be so afraid that you do not think about your life, Mary," I said, trying my best not to show the tenderness her honest reply had awakened in me, "and about what an education really means." Then I addressed them all. "I don't think any of you have learned your lessons yet. You've got to learn some dignity and responsibility and the virtue of hard work. You've got to learn that you can't behave like damned leeches and expect me to let you get away with it. I am not going to allow you or anyone at Eastside to make a travesty of the American dream. Now you continue sitting here and think about that."

All that day and the next the halls of Eastside were abuzz with reporters, and with rumors. When I wasn't being pursued by several frenetic adults armed with pads, microphones, and cameras, I was finding myself surrounded by bunches of hyper kids wanting to know if I was going to continue as their principal.

"We heard you were going to get fired, Mr. Clark."

"I heard you were going to quit."

"You can't leave Eastside, Mr. Clark. We need you."

"If they fire you, Mr. Clark, my mama's going to send me elsewhere."

"If Mr. Clark goes, we're going too!"

"They can't fire you, can they, Mr. Clark?"

"They can suspend him though. I heard they're going to suspend you, Mr. Clark, for kicking out those do-nothings. Is that true?"

"Mr. Clark ain't letting nobody push him around. He ain't leaving, because he ain't doing nothing that ain't for the good of Eastside!"

All of these sentiments were expressed over and over as I walked the halls, and parents and other members of the community were phoning in their support. This enthusiastic acknowledgment for a job well done warmed my heart. It showed me as well that I still had allies a-plenty (indeed, probably more than ever) if it became necessary to bring community pressure to bear upon the board.

"I don't know what the Board of Education has in mind," I must have said a hundred times in those few days. "I'm still trying to work things out to everyone's advantage. But go along to class and don't worry. I'm not going to let Eastside down."

The newspapers, meanwhile, tried getting the stories of the re-admitted students. The mother of one told the reporter that she agreed with me entirely. Another local paper quoted a young woman who claimed she had never been told she would need 110 credits to graduate, or that after-school tutoring was available. In fact, every Paterson eighth grader is informed on several occasions, by representatives from both city high schools of the credit system, and all Eastsiders hear of it officially at least once a year (and, unofficially, dozens of times). Furthermore, the rooms and times of after-school tutoring classes are posted at various spots throughout the building, and are regularly announced over the loudspeaker. Perhaps the girl was not fibbing. Maybe she was so often truant that she missed every pertinent announcement, and could not read the posted signs. It happens.

And perhaps editors no longer require their reporters to check the accuracy of juicy statements.

On Tuesday, with another 10 of the re-admitted returning, I moved all of these students from the auditorium to the library, and there I extended to them the possibility of eventually resuming classes. "But only after I myself review each case," I added, and left them to ponder.

It was yet another compromise move on my part. I thought the board might like it. They liked it a little, as in "the library is an improvement over the auditorium." But it was clear that the composite board would not be satisfied until I completely complied with their command of December 10. "In other words," I said to one of the teachers, "they won't rest content until those kids are back in and disrupting classes."

Then something unexpected happened. An NBC News team, part of the media blitz at Eastside, videotaped the doors of a school exit chained shut, and this was aired on the evening news. This was dynamite. The fire chief was furious, and so was the mayor.

"I like Joe Clark," said Mayor Graves. "I like what he's done for Eastside High and for all of Paterson. But I cannot allow him to get away with again chaining the doors."

I had been ordering the doors chained for years, as an efficient way of keeping the drug-dealers and hoodlums from sneaking in. This chaining the doors is a violation of the fire code. I admit that I was in violation, and I certainly don't recommend that this behavior of mine be repeated by others. Yet it was not out of negligence or in a spirit of disrespect for the law that I caused the doors to be chain-locked. Rather, I was combating a greater threat to the student body. I was keeping the hoods out.

There was a viable contingency plan in case of fire. Certain teachers, whose classrooms were close to the doors, carried the keys and could rapidly open the locks and remove the chains. The speed with which locks and chains could be removed was demonstrated on many occasions, most notably whenever anyone saw the fire inspector arriving at the school to try and catch me.

Nonetheless, it was a violation and, through a clever ruse of the inspectors, photos were taken of the chained doors in 1986. The Board of Education and I were charged, brought to court, and fined $1,000 for each of the seven illegally locked doors that they had pictures of. The penalty was waived, upon my promise that it would not happen again. Now it had happened again, and there was talk of charging me with contempt.

But before anyone goes looking for my picture on the post office wall, let me add this.

I had petitioned the board several times for electrically locked doors that could be controlled by a single switch in the principal's office. The hoods could be kept out and all the doors could be unlocked in a twinkling if need be. Indeed, with such technology available, and the perils of the inner city being as real and present as they are, it is hardly conceivable that a ghetto high school with an enrollment the size of Eastside (second largest in New Jersey) was not equipped at least five years ago with a set of such doors. Eastside still does not have them. The board, of course, has always claimed lack of funds.

Here again is the crucial issue of priorities. The board members hollered and walked all over the ceiling when news of the latest chained doors incident reached them. Predictably, their public statements emphasized that I was endangering the students. But I'd bet the real reason for their outrage was the possibility of being fined. If they had really wanted to do something to ensure the safety of the students, they would have been diligently trying to get the money for those doors. But they had not done that. How could they not have known the perilous conditions around Eastside—the violence, crime, drugs, and prostitution only a block or two away on all four sides? Oh, they knew. The papers told them, the police told them, the superintendent told them, and Joe Clark, parents, teachers, students, and shopkeepers told them. Their own eyes undoubtedly told them, when they drove along Market Street or Park Avenue in the bright light of day and beheld the dope dealers in the doorways, the thugs marauding in packs of four or five, the fur-coated pimps in their red Cadillacs and the brazen, ravaged females carrying disease up and down the pavement. They knew. Everyone knew.

And any member had only to refer to the board's records (or do a memory check) to remember how those wild streets had easily invaded, and *de facto* ruled, Eastside High in the era B.C. And they knew, if I said I needed electric doors to help keep the street out of the school, that I was telling the truth. But they did not act. They had other concerns.

Now, in that hectic December of 1987, I had the Board of Education on my back, the media in my face, and the Fire Department and the mayor at my throat. The rumor mill was working overtime. My enemies were counting me out.

Then, on Wednesday morning, another surprise. A shock. For the first time since my arrival at Eastside, a teacher was assaulted by a student.

The student was one of 10 or 15 non-achievers I had originally planned to suspend with the others. He was slated for Friday notice, but my desire to reach compromise with the board put a delay on that third group-suspension. If I had acted sooner he probably would never have bothered returning to school once booted out. He would at least have been confined to the library. Instead, this 17-year-old was moving about with the other students, his unruly nature probably pumped up by the pervasive rumors of my imminent downfall.

Because his regular English teacher was out sick that day and no substitute was readily available, the class was broken up and placed under several different teachers. This wiseguy was placed in Mrs. Gordon's class. He immediately started goofing off, jabbing other students, barking out vulgarities, throwing things. He was eventually caught flinging chalk, written up by the teacher, and escorted by the hall monitor to my office.

"You are an ingrate," I said, "and a fool. Society tries to give you an education, and you respond by throwing away your chance and using your energy to ruin other kids' opportunities." He was silent, sullen. His eyes were hard with hate. When I get through this mess, I said to myself, this punk is out for good. I signed the notice, handed it to him. "Five day suspension. Someone will call your home. Now get out of my sight, and try giving some thought to changing your ways before you end up in prison or the cemetery."

He left my office without a word, and left the building. Then he snuck around the side of the building, had an accomplice open one of the no-longer-chained doors for him from the inside, and re-entered.

Between classes, Mrs. Gordon, moving amid a large group of students, suddenly heard her name shouted in a grotesque and frightening fashion. She turned and saw the youth shoving aside surprised students, yelling profanities and violent threats, and charging at her. She cried out and tried to make it to a classroom doorway but the attacker grabbed her by the shoulders, spun her around and punched her in the face. She staggered back, instinctively threw up her arms to protect her head, and had her shoulders and arms pummeled. Screaming vulgarities the punk seized her by the neck and punched her in the stomach before two teachers and some students succeeded in pulling him away. Even then, twisting and squirming, he delivered some nasty kicks to the woman's shins.

Naturally I called the police and had the thug arrested. Mrs. Gordon, shaken up, had a few black and blue patches on her arms and legs, but was otherwise physically okay. She was greatly stunned though, as we all were, that anything like this could have taken place at the new Eastside. I was incensed.

"They stopped me from kicking the hoodlums out!" I cried. "They stopped me from keeping them out! They rile up the whole school with their pigheaded unwillingness to compromise. Then something like this happens. Is it any wonder? And they'll no doubt want to blame this on me as well!"

I decided to stop trying to compromise with the Board of Education. They were going to have to take measures against me, and I was going to blow their storm right back in their faces.

On the very next day—even as the mayor was demanding that I be held in contempt of court—the copy-cat syndrome rudely manifested itself. A 14-year-old freshman, sent to the office for rowdiness by his math teacher, Mrs. Rumsby, was suspended. But he, too, snuck back in the building and, satisfied that Clark's Eastside wasn't as strict as he'd been told, assailed the young woman, punched her in the head, and fled the building.

"No such incidents for six years," I declared on the loudspeaker, "and now, a week since the Board of Education started meddling in my affairs, we've had two assaults on teachers in as many days. I am mortified, yet I am furious. And I do not hesitate to lay the blame for both these incidents squarely at the feet of that self-righteous Board of Education. Not only do they interfere with the proper and enlightened discharge of my duties, they also expect me to take the flak for the results of their incompetence and dereliction of duty. But I utterly refuse their insidious imposition. Since they won't let me run Eastside perhaps I shall let them run it. Students and teachers, your principal is seriously considering relinquishing his position and moving on."

At my threat to resign, all that pent-up excitement permeating the school now burst into a huge and marvelous display of protest and solidarity. I was deluged by requests to stay on and I was joined by thousands of youths and adults in my resolve to win concessions from the board. An hour after my announcement, all 15 members of my administrative staff declared that they would step down if I did. By day's end more than half of Eastside's teachers (and I'm supposed to be the tyrant teachers despise) had thrown in their lot with the staff. And the students—my loving and enthusiastic students—began at once to organize a protest march on the offices of the Board of Education. They drew up a list of demands to present to the board, principally including alternative educational programs and electric-lock doors. If the board disregarded these necessities, the resolution stated, then the undersigned were prepared to leave Eastside High at once. By Friday afternoon there were 1,500 signatures on that document. And the protest march was scheduled for Monday morning.

It gave the board members something to think about over that pre-Christmas weekend. On Sunday, December 20, the chairperson phoned Superintendent Napier at his home.

"This march on the board's offices," she said, "this could be a very bad thing. Who knows, the way Clark has those kids fired up, there might be a riot. People could get hurt, and it would solve nothing. It would make matters worse."

"Maybe so," said Napier, "but what can I do about it?"

"You know him, Frank. He's your friend. Convince him to call off this madness. He'll listen to you and the kids will listen to him."

"Maybe so. But what can the board offer Clark to make it worth his while to intervene?"

"Well," she said, "we certainly don't want him to leave. Eastside needs him."

"Then what can you offer to make him stay."

"Well, we might have to take some action against him, Frank, for insubordination. But it shouldn't be anything harsh, if indeed we do decide to take action."

"And the alternative program?" asked Napier.

She sighed. "You know we've talked about this before."

"That's right. We talk and talk. We're good at that. But what about action for a change?"

"It's on the budget for next year."

"But will it stay on the budget?"

"I'll work with you to keep it on," she said.

"I'll go to Eastside first thing tomorrow."

Napier came out to the school before 7 A.M., knowing he would find me there. We talked it over.

"They're scared of the march," he said. "And I must say that it could turn into something ugly. On the other hand, if we stop it from happening, we've got a victory. A partial victory, but it's something. You've forced them to earmark money for an alternative program."

"But no doors," I said. "And they still might come after me for insubordination."

"I wouldn't put it past them. But so what? Like you've said, 'Let 'em!' You've got a concession from them, and you've got the power of the community behind you. Use that power, flaunt it. I tell you, they're scared."

"But how am I going to use it if I call off the march?"

"Just what I was considering on the ride over. You've got a crowd of excited kids here. You've got media all over the place. And you've got the superintendent here as well. Let's change the big march into a big rally, for Eastside and Joe Clark."

Which is what we did, and what a rally it was. The auditorium was packed with exuberant youngsters, and the front rows were filled with anxious reporters. Dr. Napier gave a superb speech in my support. He did me the great honor of likening my leadership to that of Martin Luther King, Jr.

"Dr. King also was forced to break some rules in those struggles for civil rights in the 1950s and 1960s," he declared. "He broke them in service to a greater cause. And he could do this without blame because he understood the cause and its righteousness. Joe Clark in the 1980s is leading the great struggle of the present day, to rescue and restructure our deteriorated educational systems. It too is a great cause, and he certainly understands its righteousness and its need. What value, after all, are civil rights if you don't possess the knowledge needed to protect and to use them? Knowledge, education—they are to the mind what food is to the body. No one can live without food, and no one can live a happy and consequential life without an education. Joe Clark understands this fully. He works and he fights to make your right to an education meaningful by making your school a place worth attending, and by insisting that each of you wakes up and works at taking full advantage of this blessing. It was bureaucratic lies and a lack of funds that pushed your principal into breaking some of the rules for your sake. Now, if we all continue to stick by Joe and his righteous cause we can expose and chase some of those lies, and make the education here at Eastside that much better.

"Joe Clark isn't going anywhere. They're not stupid enough to fire him, and we're not stupid enough to let him go. But, just in case they are that stupid, let me here and now go on record as saying, with all of you—if Joe Clark goes, so do I!"

The auditorium rocked with applause for the superintendent. It rocked and roared with great enthusiasm throughout the lengthy rally. When I walked out on stage I had a baseball bat with me. "It's a Louisville slugger," I said, "36 inches, a Willie Mays model. Willie Mays knocked quite a few baseballs out of the park in his day. Well, since I am not permitted to chain the doors shut and the board won't buy Eastside the kind of doors it needs, thugs who sneak in will meet this cleanup hitter and this Willie Mays bat. I'll knock those dope dealers and hoodlums right out of the building and clear off the property. Going, going, gone. Good-bye and good riddance. They used to call me Crazy Joe. Now they're going to call me Batman!"

(For the record, contrary to some wild rumors, I have never struck a student, or anyone, with the baseball bat. I would only use it on a hoodlum who was about to use something on me.)

The rally was an invigorating and positive event. It was evident that I had almost the whole school's support. Yet there were people in power in the bureaucracy who were determined to make this controversy my Waterloo.

On that same Monday, a Superior Court judge for Passaic County set January 7, 1988, for a non-jury, contempt of court trial for myself and the Board of Education. The board, speedy in few matters, was quite quick in informing me that I could not (being such a naughty boy) use their lawyer, but would have to hire one myself. Members of my staff, teachers, and other supporters at once organized a Joe Clark legal-expense fund. My enemies enjoyed saying that I was facing fines totalling several thousand dollars and up to six months in jail.

"I've got pals on the inside," I told one worried parent. I showed her some of the mail I'd received over the years from convicts.

"May God bless you for trying to wake those kids up to the real world," wrote one man serving time at Sing Sing. "I only wish I had had a principal or teacher like you when I was in school, someone who could have taught me the value of self-discipline, hard work and responsibility. The teachers I had didn't care. Keep up the good work."

I was still dealing with those re-admitted youths, reviewing the cases of each. I commended those who had had the courage and the will to stick it out in the library. Of them, about half were judged capable enough to re-enter classes, though only under probationary conditions: weekly evaluations and an instantly renewed permanent suspension for a cut, a truancy, or a failing grade. Those who had tried, but who I just could not in fairness to the school take back, I helped to place in vocational training courses at the community college and a local vocational school. Of those I returned to classes, all but one eventually dropped out.

On Wednesday, December 23, the Board of Education held a closed meeting to discuss the possibility of suspending me. The members emerged from the meeting saying nothing official, but spreading a new batch of rumors about the uncertainty of my professional fate. I would not be surprised to learn that spreading rumors in an attempt to frighten me was the real purpose of the meeting. All that was officially stated was that the board would discuss what actions, if any, to take against Joe Clark at its next regularly scheduled meeting in mid-January.

In other words, no more of this until after the holidays. Enjoy your Christmas. Peace.

Right. On December 29, with school out and a number of people visiting relatives, the Board of Education suddenly decided to hold a special meeting on January 4, two weeks before the regularly scheduled one. The purpose of the meeting? What to do about me. They publicly announced the open meeting only because they were required to do so. They were doing their level best to hang me as high as they could, picking a time—the

Monday after New Year's weekend—when school was out and it would be the most difficult for me to mobilize my supporters.

But my friends and I were no drunken and unaware gang of Hessians, and the surreptitious board was certainly no noble-hearted Washington.

The telephone brigade, even healthier in 1987 than it was in 1984, was soon in action. Students who had been ready to march for their principal returned to the school building during the holiday break to make big, colorful signs. One of the teachers, at his own expense, rented a bus to carry parents and students across town to Kennedy High School, where the sneak-attack meeting was to be held.

On New Year's Day, the Paterson Pastors Workshop, an organization consisting of 35 black clergymen, issued a statement avowing its firm support for Principal Joe Clark and Superintendent Frank Napier. In no uncertain language it urged the Board of Education to grant the superintendent unit-control of the finances, to provide funding for alternative education programs, and to leave the disciplining of principals solely up to the superintendent. Then these pastors prepared to join us for the big meeting.

The night of January 4 was frigid and windy. That deterred few, if any. More than 500 of my supporters, waving signs and chanting "No Joe, Don't Go!" and "He Loves Us, We Love Him!" filled the meeting room, taking all the available seats and lining up two-deep along the walls. The nine-member board took its seats on the stage, behind the long table, and looked out, with both surprise and probably a little trepidation, at the energetic Clarkian contingent.

I arrived, with my lawyer, to a great deal of applause and vocal encouragement. The purpose of the meeting was stated— Should Joe Clark be disciplined for insubordination?—and the people broke into boos and jeers. I requested the floor so that I could speak in my own defense. With the chairperson eyeing me coldly, the request was denied. My lawyer protested. She was ignored. The people jeered and complained, demanding fairness. The board responded by adjourning to a back room where, without witnesses, they voted (7 to 1, with 1 abstention) to have their lawyer draw up charges against me for insubordination. Then they returned to the stage.

Pastor LaGarde seized the microphone I had been denied and led all present in rousing choruses of "We Shall Overcome," while the sullen and angry chairperson pounded her impotent gavel. The signs and placards waved, the singing continued. Suddenly, almost inaudibly, the chairperson announced the board's kangaroo court decision and ended the meeting.

"They've accused me of not following due process," I told the crowd after that abrupt ending. "And does the Board of Education call this due process? They are cowards and weasels. They are motivated by envy and hatred."

"Why is it," asked Pastor LaGarde, "that every time we get a black leader who doesn't behave just as the power structure wants, they cut him down? We have witnessed vendetta here tonight and, I believe, bigotry as well."

I had 20 days to respond to the board's action. If I could not show sufficient reason to stop it, a suspension, if not a dismissal, would surely follow. My lawyer, however, reassured me that the board had indeed broken its own rules of procedure by not letting me speak and by not holding their vote in the open.

"We've got a sound case," she said. "We can sue them."

"Let's," I replied.

Even though the media had been on hand since the beginning of the controversy, I occasionally lost sight of the fact that Eastside and Clark were national news. On the day after the stormy meeting, however, this reality was suddenly driven home to me.

Secretary of Education William Bennett called to voice his support. The media loved it. With their ungainly equipment they followed me to the phone. They crowded around where I sat. Their klieg lights glared in my eyes. They all but salivated to know what the secretary was saying.

He said, "You've got my full support and best wishes. It's about time somebody called the bureaucracy a bureaucracy. Don't let 'em push you around, Joe. Hang tough. And I truly hope you won't quit Eastside. You're needed there. It's not only those Paterson kids who need you. We all need you there. You are a living symbol of work and hope. You are showing the country what can be done to turn our schools around."

When I got off the phone with this national figure, and looked around at the anxious newspeople, spotting ABC, CBS, NBC, and CNN on their cameras, mikes, and jackets, it re-occurred to me that I too had a bully pulpit. So I used it.

"In standing up to the Board of Education," I said, "I was standing up for all principals across the nation, many of whom lack the courage to speak for themselves. I have always only wanted to use my powers as principal to increase the chances for real education to take place. The board has consistently refused to admit that a handful of non-achievers and disrupters can spoil the education process for thousands of decent, endeavoring students. But every honest teacher knows this to be absolutely true. I am not willing to let non-learners and leeches slide through and contaminate others. I am not willing to turn out lazy heathens. I want to turn out productive citizens who will give something back to society.

"The way things at present are around the nation, we are sending the wrong message to minority kids. We're saying 'Don't worry about working hard in school, we'll give you a diploma' and 'Don't worry about getting a job, we'll give you welfare.' So minority youths, with the economic deck already stacked against them, seize upon this delinquent message as a way of just giving up. They don't work in school, and thus constantly demonstrate their academic inferiority to whites and Asians. And the bigots, and all those with racist proclivities however subtle, perceive the Hispanics and especially the blacks as racially and naturally, and therefore unalterably, inferior. It is not true, but it is the effective public perception, and it is this twisted system of hand-out education which creates it. I am against all that. I want to inspire youths to work for and truly achieve their goals. I know they can do it if they try. I did. The best way a principal can help is to create for them an atmosphere conducive to learning. That is what my task is, and I diligently perform it. I have locked horns with the board because this task, though it should be, is not high on their list of priorities, if it is there at all."

On Thursday, January 7, I was in court for the contempt charge. The Board of Education, in the person of its attorney, was there too, for the principal purpose of pointing the finger at me and, with extreme self-righteousness, whining, "It's all his fault!" Several board members, I know, were quite pleased to think that I was about to receive a painful lesson from the law, and might even go to jail. The judge, having refused my lawyer's request for a postponement, gave every indication in this first session that, seeing as how I had deliberately disobeyed the court, things would go hard for me. The court then, before arriving at a decision, adjourned until the following Monday. The board's lawyer, figuring that they were off the hook and I was on, gave me an insidious smile.

But Joe Clark has the sort of friends and allies other folk only dream about. The day before this court appearance I had received and accepted an invitation to go down to the White House, for the purpose of discussing a possible position in the Department of Education or in President Reagan's Office of Policy Development. I flew to D.C. on Saturday, not bothering to inform the board or its smiling attorney. I let them read about it in the papers.

I met with Gary Bauer, the head of the Office of Policy Development. I considered accepting the proffered post. It paid more money. It was more prestigious. Certainly I would be accorded more respect from my designated superiors, and Washington appeared a fairly nice and exciting place to live. But I turned the offer down. For one thing, I did not want to uproot my family. For another, I wanted to stay and finish my fight with the board. Most of all, there were still a number of things I wanted to accomplish at Eastside. That resuscitated institution, despite the myriad hassles, had won a place in my heart.

Bauer, however, left the door open. "If they do not have enough sense to want your services any longer in Paterson," he said, "the President will be more than happy to employ you here."

Now far be it from me to in any way suggest that people in positions of power in that dear town of Paterson, New Jersey, are at all influenced by what might be termed "political motives." Why even mention that Mr. Sombody might have said to Mr. Somebody Else, "We're going to be seen as the horses' asses of the nation, as well as bumbling fools in our town, if we stand by and let Clark get away to Washington."

"Especially," Mr. Someody Else might have replied, "if Eastside is reclaimed by the jungle, which it damn well might be."

"Might be? Will be! Then Soandso and Whatshername will have our jobs. We can't let him go!"

Or let's just say that certain people finally came to properly appreciate me. Or that the Superior Court judge was feeling uncommonly humane and benevolent that cool Monday morning, following my return from Washington. Or perhaps he had eaten something which had not agreed with him the previous Thursday. Because that doomful frown was now gone from his face, and all those foreboding indications were nowhere to be seen. I pled guilty to breaking the law, and stated my reasons. I rose and the judge blandly dropped the contempt charges, and asked for my pledge that the fire code would henceforth be followed at Eastside. I gave it. Case closed.

I noticed on the way out that the board's attorney had lost his smile, perhaps not only because of the outcome of this trial, but because the board was learning, much to its dismay, that my suit against it for illegal procedure was going to stick. Upon obtaining further legal opinions, the members were advised to drop their action against me. They did so on January 14.

"We're back to square one," their lawyer admitted. "But we are not letting this drop."

What ensued over the next six months was the shameful spectacle of the Board of Education, impelled by its Madame Chairperson, trying to do some sort of harm to Joe Clark. Toward the end of January the board resurrected its charges, then dropped them once again upon the request of the mayor, who did not appreciate all the publicity the conflict was receiving.

National publicity. I reiterated my *cri de coeur* for alternative programs on CNN's *Crossfire* in late December. My January 8 appearance on *Donahue*, in which the matter of the dismissed students was much discussed, generated more than 5,000 letters from across the nation addressed to me at Eastside High, all but 10 or 12 expressing their support. On the nationally syndicated *A Current Affair*, a call-in poll asked viewers to indicate whether they agreed with the board or Joe Clark. The result was resoundingly in my favor: 109,006 to 121. So I am not the only one sick of thugs and mealy-mouthed bureaucrats. Mayor Graves was letting the board know that they were making fools of themselves and of Paterson.

The board listened for only a little while. Toward the end of March it moved to deny me a pay raise. I appealed, and the New Jersey Principals Association provided me with a lawyer. Meanwhile, the mayor and I supported the same three individuals for election to the board. The chairperson and her allies supported three others. Each of our choices won. Weakened from within, with a lot of public egg on its collective face, the Board of Education fought my appeal throughout that summer and into the next school year. And finally lost.

But was anything won?

"Joe initiated this controversy," said Frank Napier, "because he honestly believed that if he brought the subject of the lack of alternative educational programs to the light of day, it would then be dealt with. It was, though only after a long and sometimes exasperating fight. We held the board to its promise, and a provision for an alternate program was kept on the 1988 school budget. And now what's happened? Now they are arguing about a site for the program—they will waste another year arguing. It's the usual bureaucratic runaround. But we have the program on the budget and we will, eventually, get it in place. Every principal under my jurisdiction, as well as a great number of parents and teachers, wanted such a program. Wanting alone would never have gotten it. It was only Joe who had the intelligence, the guts, and the fortitude to go out and get it. He won this program for us."

11

BUILDING UPON VICTORY

THROUGHOUT the six years of my administration, visitors to Eastside High have expressed happy surprise, if not utter amazement, at the orderliness and calm that pervades the corridors. "There's a sort of hush and buzz here," one woman, a veteran teacher from a high school in Virginia, remarked to me, as we strolled past the industrious classrooms. We had been peeking in the rooms, observing the bent heads and moving pens, the eager raised hands, or the great beauty of young, inquisitive, and attentive faces. "It's the sort of magic I sensed when first I attended the university."

"Ah, Mrs. Lamston," I said, "you flatter us."

"Not at all," she replied. "It's, it's"—she stopped to find the phrase, then smiled because it was so simple—"it's the sound of learning going on."

Simple to say. Quite another matter to bring it about.

To create that magic, to generate and maintain within the building an atmosphere conducive to learning: all of my efforts have been with that goal in mind. In previous chapters, in addition to describing how I set up my system at Eastside High, I have depicted some instances of how it works, especially in crisis situations. But the maintenance of the system, which is synonymous with the nurturing of the learning atmosphere, is a day-by-day and hour-by-hour task, not always electrified by emergencies and confrontations, nor glamorously public. Despite all the media attention we at Eastside have received over the past several years, we still work mostly in obscurity, and the bulk of what we have accomplished remains little known.

This doesn't mean that our work is beset by monotony and drudgery. It decidedly is not. The process of education is always full of obstacles to overcome. And the inner-city environment increases the difficulties. Since we are serious about education at Eastside, we do not buckle under the load; we face and name our various problems—the first step toward solving them—then follow through with well-considered actions. This persistent striving to overcome obstacles keeps things lively, and permeates our halls with that "sort of magic."

For example: One of the initial, and most crucial, problems my staff and I dealt with was the loss of classroom time. At Eastside B.C., very little learning went on. Under the tyranny of chaos and malaise, directly attributable to incompetent administration, hours upon hours of precious time were squandered. This gargantuan waste had become systemic and was bedevilling classes in all departments. We came in and, having restored order, set about rescuing those valuable minutes and returning them to their proper purpose.

Periods are 40 minutes long. Passage time between classes had been five minutes, and pedestrian traffic jams caused widespread tardiness. Kids coming into the room late—a few at a minute after period began, another at two, two at five, and another at ten minutes after, and so on—created constant, additional disruptions to situations usually already disorganized. The teacher would be taking attendance. The students, with nothing else to do, would be clowning around, fighting, dealing drugs, or wishing they were elsewhere. By the time class finally got started, ten minutes or more would have been devoured.

My method of restoring order in the corridors eliminated tardiness—indeed, we were able to cut passage time down to four minutes—and my disciplinary code cut classroom disruptions and silliness down to a minimum. But the teachers still had to use up time in taking attendance and in other necessary business. If I had let the matter end at discipline alone, time would still be wasted and the in-classroom inducement to fool around would have remained high.

But I am not strictly a martinet. I am also, and primarily, an educator. My vice-principals and I, by patrolling the corridors and looking in the classrooms, monitored the new situations our revolution had brought about. Quickly we discovered this squandered classroom time. I called a meeting of my staff and the department heads to develop a remedy.

"I am going to revive the so-called 'mental set,' " I announced. "I trust that all here present, and a majority of the teachers, have at least heard of the technique, since it was introduced to Eastside about four years ago. Mrs. Sylvani, I see you nodding your head in affirmation. Would you care to tell us what the 'mental set' is?"

"Well," she said, "the 'mental set' technique is one where the teacher has some exercise pertinent to the lesson already on the board when the students enter, so they can start work immediately and, ideally, be learning something while the teacher is taking roll."

"Exactly. And perhaps you also would not mind telling us why this technique never caught on in days past."

She smiled. "Not at all, Mr. Clark. The 'mental set' technique did not catch on because things were just too crazy to allow it to work. First it quickly became a joke, then it was quickly abandoned."

I looked around the table, making sure I met each pair of eyes. "Now, in this present administration, no matter what nicknames they have for me, things are not crazy, and the 'mental set' technique is going to work."

The department heads reacquainted their teachers with the method, and we administrators made sure to follow through. It would have been easy for teachers to apply the 'mental set' half-assedly. And some would certainly have done so, had the administration set a lazy example. In education things assuredly will go to hell if you let them. Therefore I insisted on seminars and refresher sessions.

"What we are really saying is that you use your imagination," the head of the History Department told her teachers at an after-school meeting that I, standing in the back of the room, had dropped in upon. "What you put on the board must engage and hold the students' attention. Say, for instance, you wrote, 'What were the reasons for the Boston Tea Party?' The kids might not share your interest in the event, especially if they had only covered it in homework, and you, taking roll, are not at that point able to infuse it with life. You might be more successful at getting them into it by writing, 'Would you have gone on the Boston Tea Party if you had had the chance? Give your reasons why or why not.' When finished with attendance you would then have a definite take-off point."

I also wanted every day of the school week so employed, and at once set about investigating how that matter stood.

" 'Plan loosely'!" I roared, upon first hearing that term, and having at once a sound suspicion. "What the hell do they mean by that?"

"Every teacher at Eastside knows what the term means, Mr. Clark," replied Mrs. Lopas, the head of the Foreign Languages Department, who early on brought the problem to my attention. "The previous administration used it regularly. Teachers understood that on Mondays and Fridays, at either end of the weekend, they should plan their lessons loosely—which meant, really, that they should abandon their lesson plans and teach whatever tidbits they might be able to—because it was a sure bet that not many students would be present on those days and, of those who did show, few would be in a disposition to learn anything."

"That is a contemptuous term, Mrs. Lopas," I boomed. "One that clearly demonstrates the gross ineptitude of my predecessors. Fridays and Mondays are now again part of the school week. I will in no way tolerate any teacher, student, or administrator taking it easy on those days. They are crucial days for the educational process. We can neither start nor end the week with mental slovenliness! We are not running a part-time school. I want tests and longer homework assignments on Fridays. I want reports and quizzes on Mondays. Every teacher is going to be monitored to ensure full use of those days, and of every other day. And both the teacher and the department head will be held responsible for any laxity. Anyone who plans loosely under Joe Clark had better also plan on working somewhere else!"

Very soon after my initial reforms, Eastside had real five-day weeks and full 40-minute periods. And the eight minutes we saved by cutting passage time went to study time in Home Room.

We can calculate what has been gained by totalling up the former loss of time.

With Mondays and Fridays "planned loosely," these school days were as good as lost. The record would show that, in 1981–82, Eastside held classes five days a week for nine months. In reality, classes were held only three days a week. Each of those classes was listed in the school's brochure, and in the files of the local and state Boards of Education, as lasting 40 minutes. In truth, at least 10 minutes were wasted from each class because of the archaic process of settling in and taking roll. There are seven class periods a day. That's 70 minutes a day, 210 minutes each three-day week, plus 560 minutes of planning loosely, for each of approximately 100 Eastside classes: equalling 77,000 minutes, or 1,283 hours and 20 minutes, weekly, that might have been used for learning and were not; 1,283 hours and 20 minutes fed to chaos and despair.

That means that each kid was being deprived of 12 hours and 50 minutes of learning time *each week*.

This is a conservative estimate. For a more accurate figure we would have to factor in such time-wasting, anti-educational abuses as truancy, disruptions, and teacher apathy. If such computations could somehow be made they would confirm that very little learning went on at Eastside.

The state and the district, through the boards of education, set the curricula for public high schools. Through their department heads (individuals selected by the local board), the teachers of the various required subjects are informed not only of the texts that must be used, but also of the amount of material each must cover per marking period. The department then sets, or at any rate is supposed to set, benchmarks, indicating where a teacher and his or her class are expected to be by certain days during the marking period. Ideally, the day-by-day schedule for each teacher in each class is, thus, pretty much determined.

But the ideal could never be attained in Eastside B.C. (or in most present-day inner-city schools) because—in addition to the lack of discipline and the prevalence of drugs—the syllabus-makers did not know about the 12 hours and 50 minutes per class, per student, per week, that was being frittered away. The teachers, however, knew. Not only did they have students with abominable grammar school educations, but they also had considerably less time than teachers in suburban high schools (where grammar schools are better) to try to give them high school educations.

What happened at Eastside because of this aspect of educational time-loss, and what continues to happen in inner-city schools, is that teachers rush, cram, and fake their classes through the impossible schedule.

"I was supposed to cover the American Revolution in three weeks," one teacher confided to me, once he recognized that my war against time-loss was for real. "In actuality I was doing it, or rather trying to, in half that time. I don't see how anyone learned anything. Maybe a bright kid or two took my advice and did extra reading. History already is a subject kids do not think important. How could I interest them when I was rushing through like a madman? I had to get to Yorktown, so to hell with the diplomacy of Franklin or the psychology of Benedict Arnold. It made me feel miserable, more so than the craziness in the halls. I was about to quit, but I came back to see what the 'new guy' was like."

In the Literary Masterpieces class, they skipped over *Othello* and were too shipwrecked to get to *Moby Dick*. Drama class staged, on the average, one play every two years, and that with some actors doubling, some even tripling, in roles. When the equipment in the chemistry and biology labs was not being wantonly destroyed, it was standing unused. Likewise for the Math Department's computer. The school newspaper got one issue out a year, one 4 or 6 page issue: no one from journalism class had the time, the knowledge, or the desire.

What that American history teacher did not confide to this 'new guy' was what he did about passing his bunch of hurried, uninspired, and unlearning students. I know he passed nearly all. Why, he must have thought, must I and they go through the same non-learning again? Plenty of teachers, denied the time to teach, must have reasoned in much the same sad, tragic manner. And hundreds upon hundreds of youths were passed along to the next year and on to their dummy diplomas—no education in grammar school, no education in high school, and out into the world able to offer nothing, ready only to survive by crime or handouts.

There are many economic and sociological reasons for the poor performances of minority youths both in school and out. But I believe we do not have to search far afield or wax philosophical in order to find the major culprit for time-loss in the inner-city schools. The major culprit, in nearly every case, is the principal. The competent administrator establishes order. The incompetent one does not. The competent administrator battles time-loss with energy and ingenuity, the ersatz principal ignores the problem. The principal is unquestionably the crucial figure. Should not parents be demanding the best man or woman for the job? Those are enormously important minutes that are squandered, or saved.

Another facet of this fight for learning time was the renewal of homework. Homework had not totally disappeared from Eastside High by the time I arrived, but almost. The word was used as the main component of various jokes. As in (student to teacher): "What are you gonna do to punish me, gimme some homework?" Or (teacher to teacher): "Yeah, right. I'll give 'em homework. I'll ask 'em to score me some weed." But homework is definitely not a joke, and has ceased to be thought of as one at my school.

All teachers were informed that Eastside was going to diligently follow the superintendent's stated policy on homework, which was that in every pertinent class homework should be assigned every day. The teachers were told that they would be monitored on the homework policy by their department head, by a vice-principal, and by me.

"I will be asking the students," I announced over the loudspeaker, "what their assignments were. Each one had better have something to tell me and show me." It was evident that this message was not solely for the students, and soon just as evident that I meant what I said.

"Give 'em the full half-hour's worth," I replied to one teacher who thought the superintendent's guidelines tended to load the youths down. "If a kid really does two or two and a half hours work at home in the different subjects, then he or she might actually learn something. For the college-bound student it is well that they take seriously large amounts of self-supervised study. What could be better than that they learn how to learn? For the others, they will reckon they had better do some of each assignment, because the exercises are just too big to fake. They will think that way if you unfailingly do your duty, checking them out with quizzes, oral reports, and the marking of written assignments. And I believe we will spark some desire for knowledge among the former fakers too. Don't be a softy. The most sure-fire way to show compassion for them is to show 'em no mercy now."

I also resuscitated the term paper and long-range project. At a faculty and staff meeting, about five weeks into my first year, we discovered that term papers or research papers had not been assigned at Eastside High for about three years.

"I'd lay 3 to 1 to anybody in this room," said one teacher, "that 9 of the first 10 students you'd ask would not know what a term paper was." He got no takers, and would not have gotten one at midnight in Atlantic City.

"What was the use of assigning them anymore?" someone else commented. "Nobody would do them. And they didn't care if you tried to discipline them. They knew you couldn't. And they knew you probably wouldn't fail them either. They were laughing at us. I remember one girl, who was probably drunk, telling me that it didn't matter who wrote this damn book or that damn book. 'I'm gonna watch everything on the TV anyhow!' she said. And the whole class laughed their asses off. I could not have assigned those demons a comic book!"

"Exorcising the demons," I said, "that's my job, and all of you can see that I'm doing it. In this instance, your job, as teachers, is to bring back the term paper, the classic term paper that each of us had to labor at several times in our student years. Perhaps some teachers have forgotten what a term paper consists of. I suggest they start remembering."

"Mr. Clark, may I say something?"

"Please do," I said to the teacher who had chimed in.

She was a slight English instructor, with more than 30 years of experience, most of it at Eastside. She had known the school before the deterioration, through all the years of the disgrace, and was now happily witnessing Eastside's renaissance. "Not too long ago," she said, "I was visited by a former student of mine from many years ago. He had made a fine success for himself in the business world, a vice president somewhere or other, and was the breadwinner for a lovely family. He showed me the pictures. And what he said to me was, 'When you taught me how to do a term paper, you taught me everything I needed to know. When I went to college all my studies had to do with research, references, clear denotation. Countless times I thanked God and you for teaching me these skills and impressing upon me their importance. Learning that one thing in high school was the reason I did well in college.' "

"Thank you, thank you for sharing that wonderful anecdote with us," I told the teacher. I was truly pleased, and moved. "Did you hear that? Did everyone hear that marvelous story? That man most probably owes his success and happiness to being taught how to compose a term paper. It is a truly beautiful and hopeful thing. Wake up, teachers and administrators, take heed of what you can bring about through diligently pursuing your vocation. You can turn lives around. It is what you are here to do. It is the task at hand. Discard your cynicism. You may hold the key to some human being's future happiness. And that possibility should certainly inspire you to do your utmost. If it doesn't inspire you, then you truly are in the wrong line of work. But if it does, be assured that you now have a principal who will allow you to act on your inspiration. Enough talk. Two long-range projects a year for every alpha class, at least one being a classic research paper, and one long-range project for every other class. I want the first ones assigned before the month is out."

As these various changes began to operate, and the chaotic muddles that had passed for classes at Eastside B.C. began to take on order and clarity, a certain type of student became noticeable. The forgotten student, the neglected student, the underrated student. He or she needed some special help or guidance, which need formerly went undetected, like an appleseed in a mudslide. Now such needs could be perceived and addressed. He or she was intelligent, more intelligent in fact than anyone had ever realized. In the new Eastside atmosphere that intelligence could shine. It gives me unspeakable joy to see that this young man or that young woman is being recommended by a teacher for a higher track, and an even greater pleasure to learn, by studying the record, that I can legitimately approve the recommendation.

"One more kid for college," I have several times commented while handing the form to the department head, "one less for the penitentiary."

There is little exaggeration in that statement. The jungle world of the inner city devours potential like lions would a defenseless fawn. For the capable yet beset, distrustful, resentful, unclear, and quicksilver mind of an inner-city youth, the timely and proper inducement a well run classroom provides can make a lifetime of difference.

Eastside's College Prep classes have noticeably increased in enrollment since our regime came in. We now have more students taking the SAT tests, and our SAT scores have inched up since 1982. We also show a parallel, slight yet steady increase in students going on to college, and this in a period (1980 to 1988) when college enrollment nationwide for minorities (black and Hispanic) was down by 50 percent.

I do not claim spectacular advances in this area. Our advances in College Prep have been modest but real, and there are numerous, encouraging success stories from Eastside's college students. But College Prep is only one curriculum among five. The majority of our students are enrolled in Business Education, Home Economics, and Industrial Arts, and a smaller proportion is in Fine Arts (music and art). I, naturally enough, would like to see enrollment in College Prep and Fine Arts increase, not because I am an elitist, but because I think the present breakdown disproportionate. But I realize that we of Eastside are just now climbing out of two decades of terrible social, economic, psychological, educational, and spiritual decay and stagnation. The aspiration for higher learning is slower to revive than I would like. Nonetheless, there is much here to make me rejoice and be proud.

Our graduates are ready and able to snap the ghetto's vicious cycle and become good, productive citizens.

I dare say that these are not the sort of young men and women coming out of the vast majority of inner-city high schools, nor, to a significant degree, are they the sort now coming out of most high schools, urban, suburban, or rural. But the youngsters coming into Eastside are, with some noteworthy exceptions, in as anti-educational a condition as any group of kids from Watts or the South Side of Chicago.

The bulk of our students come to us from inferior grammar schools, inner-city grammar schools where order has broken down and teaching has deteriorated. All have to some degree been tainted by the street, and many are directly acquainted with drugs, crime, and other perversities. Their priorities are topsy-turvy. Their attention spans are miniscule. Their scholastic abilities are absolutely horrendous, with average reading capability at fourth grade level. In former times these societal barbarians would simply have been processed through, exiting high school as functionally illiterate as when they entered, and a good deal more barbaric. Eastside under Joe Clark turns these youngsters around. Quite literally, we civilize them.

Upon entry every freshman is required to take the State-standardized High School Proficiency Test, which samples abilities in the 3 R's. Invariably the majority of our students fail in at least one category, and a disturbing number in two or all three. Because no one can be graduated who does not achieve three passing marks in the H.S.P.T., students re-take whichever test or tests they have failed. This occurs the following year after they, by state requirement, have undergone basic skills courses in the problem subjects. Imagine how many basic skills these kids— especially those considered stupid—learned in the days of wild corridors, "plan loosely," and wasted hours. The students faced a different and, by all accounts, much easier state-issued test in those years (called the Minimum Basic Skills Test). Yet the rate of repeated failure, and the number of test-frustrated dropouts, was higher then than now. It is a shame that we at the high school level should be forced into teaching kids the skills they should have learned in grammar school, but at least now, at Eastside, we do accomplish this extra and necessary task. And then some.

"Walter!" I boomed one afternoon over the bullhorn to a young man a corridor away. "Walter Adams, come and see me at once."

He came, a bit apprehensively. I waited a few moments, for the corridors to empty into the classrooms, then said, "I see you're taking Basic Computational."

He hung his head. "Yes, Mr. Clark. I failed the math proficiency test."

"But you plan to pass it sophomore year?"

He straightened up. "Oh yes, Mr. Clark. Absolutely!"

"Absolutely, eh? Then there must be some mistake, because I

didn't see your name on the list for H.S.P.T. class on Saturdays."

He stared along the empty hall. "I didn't sign up."

"No?"

"I don't need to, Mr. Clark. I'll learn all I need in Basic, and I like my Saturday mornings, you know."

"And what do you do on Saturday mornings, Walter, that you like them so much? What do you do? Lie in bed and watch cartoons?"

He blushed and stared at the floor. My guess had hit the bull's eye. It's a knack you develop when you are around kids so many years, and it adds that much more power to your words. "Walter," I continued, "what happens if you don't pass the proficiency test next year."

"I'll have to take it again, junior year," he mumbled.

"What else?"

"I'll have to take Basic again."

"And?"

He pondered it, shook his head. "I don't know, Mr. Clark. What?"

"You obviously do have trouble with math, Walter. You are forgetting to subtract the 5 credits you won't be receiving for this year's Basic if you flunk the test. And you are forgetting the extra work you will have to do in the next few years to make up those credits and graduate. Why not do yourself a big favor, skip Looney Tunes and sign up for the Saturday course."

He looked down and up, this way and that, shoving his hands in his pockets, shuffling his feet. Finally he gave me a sly glance. "You're not saying I have to sign up, are you, Mr. Clark?"

I frowned my most authoritarian frown. "No, Walter, I am not saying you have to. It's a voluntary course, just something we provide for students who need and want help. I guess it will just take up too much of your cartoon time, be too much work. Forget I brought it up. Get yourself a late pass at the office."

I turned and walked. Later that week he signed up for the Saturday class. The following year he passed the test. I shamed him, I imagine, into acting more responsibly regarding his education and his future. He could have skulked away from my challenge but, because his solicitous principal went after and prodded him, he did the more grown up thing. He passed a solitary test, for which no statistics are available, but which is ultimately more important than the H.S.P.T. Furthermore, when his calculator breaks or the computer is down, he will know how to add.

We are always challenging all of them. With discipline, with good examples, with vigorous classroom periods, with homework and term papers, with full accountability for their actions both academic and social. We are relentless, because I, cracking the whip, am relentless.

Every morning over the loudspeaker I teach them vocabulary. "The words for today are 'scintillate' and 'martinet.' " I spell them, give their principal meanings, then use each in a sentence: "Our Honor Roll students simply scintillate with knowledge" and "Our beloved principal makes a martinet look like a softy."

A happy number of youngsters remember the words. I hear them using them in the corridors; they pop up in written assignments. Several teachers have directly attributed an increased use of dictionaries to my daily practice. That warms my heart. That is a victory indeed.

One female student asked me if the Board of Education was an oligarchy.

"Indubitably," I replied.

Now and then, just to keep students, teachers, department heads, and vice-principals on their toes, I pop in and teach a class myself.

"What's your biggest problem with this subject?" I asked a freshman, after assuming command of an English class.

"Paragraphs, Mr. Clark," he said. "I can't write 'em."

"Yes you can. You just haven't learned how yet." I took a desk next to the young man, set out a sheet of paper before me, took up a pen and poised it. "Now you get ready just as I am," I said. He did. "And when you have the pen ready to write, just like that, then do not write a word. That is, until first you close your eyes and think about what you want to write. Think the paragraph through in your mind, from beginning to end, each sentence of your thought. Then after you've got it straight in your head, open your eyes and put it on paper. That's how to do it. Thought first, then action. Ever try that method before?"

"No, Mr. Clark."

"Give it a try. Practice it. If it works for you, then, well, you know what?"

"What, Mr. Clark?"

"Then you've learned something."

In addition to our regular curricula we offer dozens of supplemental programs. They tend not only to extend the educational atmosphere in time (before and after classes) and space (out into the community), but also to greatly color and enrich it. There are work-study programs in a wide range of skilled and semi-skilled occupations, in business machinery and office procedures, in marketing, in many hospital and laboratory positions, in child-care and home services, in textiles and fashion, in food services. In one such program, several of the participating firms have felt it to their advantage to help finance certain students who want to go on to college. Another program, called CHOICES, permits students undecided about their careers to sample various jobs, giving the much needed (and, I think, justly deserved) opportunity to make a sound, informed decision on a matter so very important.

We have a computer club, a job seeking club, and a forensics club, to name a few. The school newspaper now cranks out an issue a month. We have also begun peer-tutoring, a companion to our older tutoring program, for youths who feel more comfortable and able to learn around other (qualified and approved) youths. And there are peer-homework groups at work.

Funding for programs outside the approved curriculum is usually forthcoming from involved businesses, not because of the Board of Education, but because of my efforts. Our teachers, administrators, and parents work on a volunteer basis. They are usually as serious about making these various projects meaningful as I am about maintaining order and the learning environment. Or, anyway, almost as serious.

Once a year, in the spring, we celebrate Career Day, when numerous businesses set up booths around the school, meet with students, and inform them of the current opportunities and requirements. We solicit as much straight-shooting material as possible. Career Day survives on contributions.

In the fall we have a College Day. It is less a celebration, not because we think it less important, but because college representatives are at the school on most other days, ready to speak with the interested students. Also, material on almost all the colleges is in the library.

Some of these programs I rejuvenated, some I invented, and some were simply dropped in our lap because of the publicity Eastside and I have received. The most prominent of this latter category is the scholarship program started up through a grant from a computer company from Fort Lee, New Jersey.

"Hello, Mr. Clark?" said the voice over the phone.

"Yes."

"My name is Jack Berdy. I'm the chairman of Online Software, Inc. You don't know me, sir. But my associates and I admire you, and we'd like to give your high school a million dollars."

I believed that as much as I had believed my secretary when, several years ago, she said the President of the United States was on the line for me. "Stop joking and get back to work!" is what I told her. But Mr. Reagan was on the line. And Mr. Berdy was on the level.

The program involves a review board of administrators, teachers, and a parent, who carefully study the applications of numerous students, and choose five a year, each of whom will receive a four-year college scholarship. Online's only condition to the grant was that those receiving scholarship money must be majoring in a subject dealing with or directly related to computers. We already have our first five candidates.

Then there was this little story:

My pastor, the Reverend LaGarde, introduced me one day to a man who was anxious, he said, to shake my hand. Well, I have shaken a lot of hands, so I shook another. The man, named Vincent, seemed genuinely pleased to meet me and, while I secretly feared that he was going to try to sell me insurance, he began telling me of his work.

"I was working as a placement officer at CPI, Computer Processing Institute, in Paramus," he said. "My job was to interview and assess the aptitudes of different applicants to the school, and so help to place them in the one of our four programs most suited to their abilities. I have met a lot of people in this connection. Most of them are young people, who are, supposedly at least, looking for something better than what they have been handed.

"A major trouble was, however, that often the young person who sat across the desk from me did not seem to care enough about himself or herself or the future to take the few common sense steps to help him earn a placement. I mean so many dressed sloppily, were poorly groomed, seemed distracted and resentful, came late, and projected the attitude that any job was nothing less than hell itself and why should they have to suffer Adam's curse.

"This was a career training opportunity, and in a dynamic field where there is high demand, room to advance, job security, and the chance to make quite good money without breaking your back. But so many of these youths did not seem at all to grasp this. It was as though coming to me was just one more boring and unfair thing they were being forced to do. The grimaces were the ugliest and the whinings the loudest when they learned they would have to take a test. What torture could possibly be worse? I lost a great many right there. I used to tell them straight out that this might be their best, last, or only real chance. I meant it, but I was seldom understood.

"On the other hand there were certain young people, a minority to be sure, who were the antithesis of these immature and disorganized youths. They were well-dressed and groomed, interviewed well, asked pertinent questions, had no problems with being on time or taking a test, and seemed altogether serious about considering computer work for a career. They listened and understood the distinctions when I explained the different study programs. It was a pleasure to place them, as well as an honor to the school to have them. Needless to say, they've done exceedingly well at CPI, and afterwards.

"The contrast between these two sorts of youths was very pronounced. It astounded me, though something soon became very evident. Again and again on the application form of the well-prepared young person the high school attended was Eastside in Paterson. I had never before heard of Eastside High, nor of you, Mr. Clark. But I surmised that it must be a unique institution, and so I looked into it and have come to shake your hand and congratulate you on so outstanding an accomplishment. Over the last year CPI has had an enrollment of 1,100 new students from all over northern New Jersey. Ninety of our successful applicants were from your school."

It was as personally rewarding to hear that as it was to receive the million dollars.

12

THE SPIRIT THAT MOVES US

I WENT looking, that Wednesday morning before the homeroom bell, for my singer. I stepped out into the corridor, into that vivacious, tittering flow of students talking and laughing, rattling lockers, saying hello.

"Hey, Terence, my man!" I called to a thin fellow chatting with some pretty girls. "You're today's opening act. One minute to curtain time."

The girls giggled. Terence's face lit up. Hurriedly he made his way across the packed corridor. "But Mr. Clark, Mr. Clark!"

"No excuses."

"No excuses, Mr. Clark," he said. "I want to sing. But we got a group."

"Is that right? And who is in this group?"

"Me and Marvin and Tony and Jack. We're smooth, Mr. Clark. We're cool."

"What's your group's name?"

He smiled proudly, "The Blue Ghosts!"

"I like it." The Ghost is Eastside's emblem, the school colors

163

are orange and blue. "Your group is on right after Mrs. Maus' announcements."

"All right!" he cried, just as the bell rang, then hurried off to find the other three.

In a little more than a minute they were in the office, crowding around the P.A. system's microphone as our executive vice principal stepped away. I walked over and announced them. "Today's rendition of Eastside's alma mater will be performed by the Blue Ghosts," I said. Then I gave Terence the nod.

They leaned over, snapping their fingers and, with passable four-part harmony, in a style reminiscent of the Temptations, sang:

> Fair Eastside,
> by thy side we'll stand
> and always praise the name
> To ever lend our hearts and hands
> To help increase thy fame
> The honor of old Eastside High
> brings forth our loyalty:
> So cheer for dear old Eastside High
> Lead on to Victory

They finished with some bass scat and a sort of ululation. Smiles circulated around the office. It was amusing enough. But this performance, as with every singing of the alma mater, had a serious side as well. For one thing, any student challenged who cannot sing the school song faces suspension for the remainder of the day. And it is a useful mnemonic for scores of kids who have never before memorized anything even vaguely connected with education—though they could reel off the lyrics to three or four dozen pop songs, as well as the positions, batting averages, and home run totals for every one of the New York Mets. The kids learn, out of the fear of my wrath and the prospective embarrassment of facing their peers (my allies), to commit to memory the alma mater. Suddenly they have no excuse for not knowing the first six (or last six) U.S. Presidents, the chemical symbol for carbon dioxide, or the parts of a sentence. Most importantly, this adult emphasis on the school song fosters serious pride in the school and all that it stands for.

"Not bad," I said to them. "But I think you had better be sure to learn your math and English, so you can find work, in case there's any delay with the record contract."

They took my comment in good humor. "You mean we might be ahead of our time, Mr. Clark?" said Marvin.

"Look at these, Mr. Clark," cried Tony, yanking up a pant leg, to reveal bright orange socks with a blue top band.

"I've got the colors too," said Terence, in blue shirt and orange belt.

"Me too!" Marvin chimed in.

"Very good, Ghosts, very good," I said, ushering them to the door. Every Wednesday is school colors day. Students are encouraged, though not required, to display the orange and blue. One of the gym teachers, who had just come in, commented that:

"When I first came to Eastside, in 1980, people didn't even know what the colors were, let alone the alma mater. The football uniforms were blue and gold, and the cheerleaders were singing 'Hurray for the orange and blue!' Year after year they ordered those same uniforms. I mentioned it. 'Who cares?' was the reply. Some school spirit, eh?"

School spirit. Eastside High now abounds in it. But for us it goes beyond the alma mater, the marching band, and the Thanksgiving Day football game. The spirit at Eastside before the Clarkian revolution was demonic and self-destructive. Now it is conducive to education and self-esteem.

One of my interests is gardening, and sometimes I view Eastside as a garden. At Eastside, we did not come into a garden already arranged that had merely suffered from some neglect and bad taste. What we came upon was a fire-blasted patch of brown and cracked earth. Nothing grew there but noxious weeds. We faced the extremely difficult task of returning this poor patch to cultivation. We did so, and learned that, along with the difficulty, came the freedom of growing just the sort of garden we wanted. We nurtured our garden of Eastside High, from roots to blossoms, to full colorful bloom, with a solid, new, proud spirit.

School spirit is not merely symbols and ritual. It is not merely tradition. The traditional re-enactment of symbol and ritual in many schools is often the empty husk of a spirit that has not been nurtured or reinvigorated. School spirit is closely akin to the spirit of learning. It is the spirit of effort and attainment, of aspiration and enthusiasm, of curiosity and the joy of discovery, of stick-to-itiveness and optimism. It is the spirit of camaraderie, of the budding understanding of common needs and desires, and of the mutual respect for individual differences. It is the building of self-esteem, the fostering of sanity. It is the awakening of brotherhood and sisterhood and the conquering of prejudice and hate. It is the beginning of the recognition of this blessed opportunity to learn and become a contributing part of a civilization built through human genius, toil, courage, and blood.

Genuine school spirit can serve as an able midwife to something we are nowadays so lacking, the spirit of family. It can translate into the spirit of neighborhood, of community, of patriotism, and of a humane world view. It can be a prelude to these noble states because it is so intimately connected with sound growth, with the mature passage into adulthood, with all facets of that crucial process we call education.

Spirit is the necessary companion to school discipline. Neither can exist without the other. Without discipline, school spirit would quickly deteriorate into horseplay and wildness. Without spirit, discipline is mere regimentation—dry, soulless, and resented. Discipline alone would breed eventual rebellion. Discipline alone would never stir the hearts of both the teachers and the students, and would therefore never reach out and stir the community. But the disciplined and spirited energy of Eastside High does just that, every day.

Did you ever walk through a depressed urban area and suddenly see a group of youths approaching, five of them, maybe ten, blocking the sidewalk and spilling off into the street? How did you feel, or how would you feel? Secure? Would it help much that it was daylight and these apparently were school kids? Or would those facts just add irony to your mounting fear? Perhaps you are not a big, imposing person. Perhaps you are a well-dressed office worker, with cash in your wallet, painfully aware of looking more affluent than you are. Or maybe you are a woman alone, or a mother with an infant and a toddler. Or a person of another race, an old person, or a defenseless kid. What do you do?

Run away? Freeze? They're loud and vulgar, and they have

certainly spotted you. Perhaps you cross the street and have your ears stung by obscene taunts. Probably you muster your dignity and proceed forward. Still—even if you are not robbed or hit or sexually abused—you will probably be forced to step aside, and be treated to threats and curses. Even as your limbs weaken with fear, your cheeks burn with anger and shame for having been intimidated in the midst of an ostensibly civilized society, and on the streets of your own city or your own neighborhood.

This sort of barbarous little drama goes on every day on poverty-scarred streets the nation over. But it does not happen in the neighborhoods of Eastside High, at least not involving our students. Not any more. The few bullies remaining in our school would not dare to behave like that, not only because they know that the story probably will reach me, but also because the vast majority of the student body rejects such disgraceful antics. Bullies who meet substantial opposition and lack even a small audience will attempt very little. More significantly, our students are proud of the honorable reputation the school has earned, and have begun to perceive how their decent behavior has a reciprocal effect in the home and the community.

A mother called one morning simply to let me know that the comportment and positive attitude of her oldest boy, a freshman at Eastside, was being adulated and copied by his two younger brothers, both of whom were attending a rather non-educational grammar school.

"The change is really remarkable," she said. "They dress neatly for school. They no longer wear the sideways baseball caps, or pal around with the little hoodlums who sell drugs for the bigger dealers. Roger and his friend Paul, who's a sophomore at Eastside, talk to the younger kids about the dangers of drugs, and about the need for a good education. Now my younger ones don't try staying out 'til all hours. Now they want neat covers on their books, and stick-on subject tags. They even do their homework when Roger sits down to do his. My little Elliot just yesterday told me he wanted to be a lawyer. Believe me, Mr. Clark, I have more than once reckoned that one day he would be *needing* a lawyer. It's remarkable. And of course both of them want to go to Eastside."

More than discipline and academics are at work here. That's

school spirit. Those kids are going to be assets, not threats, to the community. As are the Eastsiders who travel inoffensively to and from school, frightening no one except the pigeons. Or those who frequent the pizza parlors and sweet shops, or stop in the supermarket or dimestore; decent kids, living proof of the success of our revolution.

Seven or eight (or ten or fifteen) years ago, store-owners and managers shuddered when kids from the high school pushed through their doors. Fights broke out in the restaurants in those days, obscenities and defacements were daily fare. Customers and employees were intimidated and assaulted. Shoplifting, vandalism, armed robbery—all were common. Drugs were dealt either in the store or just outside. There were never enough police to deal with the problems. Merchants and store managers not only had to contend with a loss of customers and the threat of physical violence, but also with rising insurance rates.

As was true of the chaos within the school at Eastside B.C., this neighborhood malevolence stemmed from a relatively small bunch of bad apples among the student body who hung around with the drug-pushing criminal element. It thrived on the streets in a morbid atmosphere of apathy and helplessness. The good youths (which is to say most of them) lived in fear and despair, with recourse to various contrivances of jungle survival. The school, which little enough existed for the students during the day, ceased all connection with them after 3 P.M., while school and community played a sorry game of mutual avoidance. But the spirit of the new Eastside flowed out to the surrounding neighborhood, through the active agency of the rejuvenated students. It steadily won converts. The new message was trumpeted forth by their improved behavior. It gradually became evident to residents and merchants that the focus for these young people had switched from drugs and crime to success in life through diligent striving. The criminal element lost much of its market and had to look elsewhere. Residents felt safer because they were safer. Merchants were happier, because their stores were no longer hassle zones. Eastside youths are no longer associated with hoodlums. They are associated with decency, and are welcome throughout the neighborhood.

I have never subscribed to the heresy that school begins at 8:30 A.M. and ends at 3 P.M. The notion that the school building is nothing more than a factory and the students mere products turned out by an assembly line shows an abominable misunderstanding of the whole process of education. In the more affluent communities the consequences of such a blind approach might not be readily discernible, but the consequences are still perilous, because wrongheadedness is passed along to the next generation.

When such a rift exists between the school and the other aspects of suburban life, the student is likely to regard high school education as only the obtaining of a diploma, a ticket to college, which in turn is seen as nothing more than a ritual that must be suffered through in order to start a well-paying career. Meanwhile, when these rituals are acted out in an anemic spirit of school and home and neighborhood, the actual education our children absorb is that of the self-centered non-intellectual materialism they see all around them: the world of designer clothes, country clubs, BMWs, and Jacuzzis, the world of alcohol, infidelity, apathy, and cynicism. They learn to connive and seduce, and to use human beings like disposable toys. They learn a shadow-dance of life, projecting false images, piling up mere objects, and paying psychiatrists to protect them from their consciences. They become the lawyers who do not acknowledge the existence of right and wrong, the advertising people who lie, the Wall Street *enfants terribles* who wreck lives and the economy itself for their own short term fortunes, the politicians who embrace criminals to stay in power, and the parents who pass on this vacuity of soul to yet another generation.

As the Baron de Montesquieu pointed out 240 years ago, the education youths receive from the world obviates what they are taught at home and in school.

What in many cases these youths do not learn is morality. That is, a sense of fairness to serve as a guide for their actions. The schools could teach them this, if the schools were run with the right intentions, the right spirit. I am not suggesting the removal of the separation of church and state. What I am saying is that education, properly understood and practiced, requires an energetic commitment from teachers and administrators not only to provide career skills, but also to elevate the mind and the heart to the whole story of life; its wonders and dangers, its joys and sorrows, its struggles and possibilities. The dynamic of right and wrong runs throughout this whole story—from Lexington to Los Alamos, from Hippocrates to Macbeth, from the earliest myths to the headlines of this morning's newspaper—and the truly dedicated teacher cannot help but project the rightness of his or her task, which is the genuine preparation of the next generation for the challenge of life. After all, for a sane, mature adult (which, I will be so bold to declare, a teacher ought to be) to make a thoughtful commitment to education, a functioning morality is required: he or she wants to better the human condition.

The dedicated administrator must always act with energy, acumen, and judgment—which is to say with spirit. He or she will know that lethargy, boredom, and woodenness of routine can be as detrimental as drug use. Good teachers can move the students. The good principal must reach out and move the whole community, let students, parents, and businesses know that the school is not just 8:30 to 3:00, but a vital and vibrant part of their lives.

That sort of spirited education will teach students morality just as the everyday speech of grown-ups teaches language to infants. Indeed, that is the best way to instill a sense of justice, common purpose, and compassion: by example rather than by dogma.

In the inner city the disastrous consequences of the 8:30 to 3:00 mentality are more visible. Here most kids have nowhere to go to stay out of harm's way. If the school doors shut on them, they find that the golden doors to the temple of materialism are shut as well. Yet, having basically the same idols as the suburban youths, the inner-city kids try the temple's back door. They go after the fancy clothes and the BMWs not through their parents' bank accounts, but via crime, mainly drug trafficking. It's a wilder and more dangerous road, often ending in the prison cell or the early grave.

In an inner-city school, the spirit must be strong enough to deliver right away. The kids we're trying to reach get more twisted and incorrigible by the hour. The educators, especially the principal, must be ready to do battle for students' souls. When the administrator has the will and ability to meet this challenge, a true school spirit will flow forth and baptize that institution for a brighter day. This is why every facet of my no-

nonsense method of running Eastside is flavored with a heavy dose of school spirit.

The good repair and cleanliness of the building; the guards outside and the teachers monitoring the corridors; the pitching out of unruly students and troublesome teachers; the strictly enforced discipline; the reaching out through the churches; the rejuvenating of the Home School Councils: the salvaging of hours of learning time; the abundance of support programs; the bullhorn, the baseball bat; school spirit enlivens and empowers all these things, and is, in turn, fueled by each. The kids bring the spirit home with them. Supportive parents pump the spirit back into the school. They are inspired, we are further inspired, and each of our commitments (to teach, to learn, to supervise, to assist) is strengthened.

In 1986, an NBC news team was here, working on Connie Chung's special about Eastside and myself (which proved to be the media story that eventually led to the film, *Lean on Me*). During a coffee break, one of the NBC production people said to me, "I've got to congratulate you. I'm a skeptic by nature, and was prepared to be unimpressed. But this is the real thing. I mean, there's a positive feeling throughout this whole place. Kids look like they're happy to be here. Teachers tell me they're glad to be able to do their jobs. This just isn't your ordinary 1980s high school."

"It ought to be, sir," I said. "It really ought to be."

"It reminds me of my high school, in the mid-1960s," said another member of the crew. "I went to a Catholic school. This school has the same sense of peace, but it's more exciting, as though the kids here are more aware of what a good deal they've got."

"They have the ghetto all around them, often in their homes," I replied. "They love Eastside like a savior. They know that, in addition to giving them traditional education, we are working to address their needs and fill the voids in their hard-pressed lives. They have all heard empty promises before, and are expert at sniffing out hypocrisy. But they love us because we are, as you've said, the real thing. We are always willing to go the extra mile."

For example. The City of Paterson has a drug awareness program that functions in all its schools. Cities and towns throughout the nation have similar well-intentioned and rather anemic programs. Drug use, meanwhile, increases. Eastside, of course, participates in the Paterson program. But we don't stop at pamphlets and the occasional lecturer.

Three police officers who had, before my arrival, spent much of their time at Eastside, tracking down drugs, gangs, and weapons were particularly impressed with how quickly and efficiently I had run the drug dealers out. Suddenly, there was no longer a need for their daily (even weekly or monthly) visits, but they were taken with the awakened spirit of the new Eastside.

"Mr. Clark," said one, "we are knocked out by what you have done and are continuing to do. In fact, we'd welcome the chance to be a part of it."

"You've removed the drugs from the school," said another, "but these kids have to go home every day to neighborhoods and homes where drug use is still rampant. But since things have quieted down here at Eastside, maybe we could use that quiet to inform the kids of all the dangers of narcotics."

That was the start of Eastside's unique Brothers in Blue program. It was not ordered or suggested by the board or the superintendent or any outside agency, but grew out of a sincere desire of these individuals to help underprivileged and endangered youths, and out of the new spirit prevalent at the school which declared that their time would not be spent in vain. These three dedicated officers (one was a Sister in Blue) continued to come to Eastside regularly, at least one every day. On some days they addressed an assembly of students. More often they would speak in the health classes. Along with a great deal of pertinent information about the biological and legal ramifications of drug use, the kids heard dozens of personal accounts of the horrors of the street, the hospital wards, and the prison: the 40-year-old addict, the OD in the alley, the teenage girl caught in a crossfire, the young prisoner who became the property of another. The officers laid it on the line to the students—truth is essential in the battle for souls—and at times there were tears in the eyes of both listeners and speaker.

It was Eastside's spirit as well as its discipline that brought the officers there to teach. And it was the heartfelt spirit of the officers that touched the students and turned a significant number of lives around.

All Paterson schools have, at least ostensibly, counseling for drug-troubled students. At Eastside, however, we offer what none of the other schools do. Always, during school hours, there is at least one designated adult (teacher or administrator) available in the building whom the troubled student can speak with at once. The door is always open. The meeting takes top priority. It will never be postponed or even delayed. If two needful students show up at the same moment, another adult will be provided.

"More than once," explained a member of our Guidance Department, "I have had a youth battling a drug or alcohol dependency, who felt especial anxiety—stemming from home, or school, or peers, or somewhere else—and more pressure than he thought he could endure. He came to me and we talked about it: how everybody has problems now and again, how the mature thing is not to lean on any substance, and how even as we spoke he was building strength for future resistance. That sort of thing. On the street it's an easy matter to meet a connection to purchase dope and ruin your life. The idea here is to give the youth just as ready a connection for saving his or her life."

A bandleader makes sure that every musician is taking care of his or her instrument. A coach keeps an eye on every player to see that each is game-ready. The able administrator is tireless in his solicitude for every student in his charge. School spirit, to be genuine, must flow from the group to the individual and back again.

Every morning, without fail, along with the vocabulary lesson and the various commendations of deserving students, I use the P.A. system to remind them all how important this day of their education is. And I stress the need for both self-esteem and self-discipline.

"The reason for discipline," I have said more than once, "is not only the maintenance of order. The discipline of Eastside High is meant, as well, to teach each of you self-discipline. Self-discipline is how adults get things done, important things especially. When you have self-discipline you can compete effectively in the world. You can set high standards for yourself, overcome the intervening obstacles, and attain your goals. Self-discipline will allow you to truly believe in yourself. Let's not fool ourselves. We are, almost all of us, minority individuals, and therefore have a tougher row to hoe. I am not saying this so that you will whine and feel sorry for yourselves, like little babies. I am definitely not handing you an excuse. There are no excuses for not doing your best. What I am presenting you with is a challenge. When you depart Eastside High and enter into the adult world, you must be prepared for the rigors of the struggle of life itself. Yes, of course, it is necessary and good to have the knowledge and skills to survive and advance, and each of you ought to be studying hard with that in mind. But I also want you to have something else, something even more necessary and good. Self-discipline. It is the staunchest ally, the truest friend. It is the key to survival and success."

A motivational message every morning. I do not let up, because the street (the jungle) is too close at hand, and it never lets up. Furthermore, Joe Clark is a proven commodity: the kids believe me and trust that I have their best interests at heart. This is what makes the words worth something. This is school spirit, indeed.

Nevertheless there are youths attending Eastside whose home environments and life experiences thus far have been so inimical to the natural and civilized processes of development, that the spirit which moves through each Eastside day, touching most of the student body and the staff, does not sufficiently motivate these unfortunates to shoulder their personal burdens and carry on. We have always been on the lookout for any aberrations or prospective problems. Early on in our regime we began to pick out those kids who were unduly distracted, depressed, and merely going through the motions. We began to reach out to them with special programs.

Choose Life is the program to assist any youngster so down-trodden and depressed as to consider suicide. Trained individuals, usually from our Guidance Department, respond to calls for help from teachers, parents, the youths themselves, or whomever, and, working with the school psychiatrist, do whatever it takes to turn the youth away from the tragic course. And they probe for the roots of the problem. Sometimes it can be handled by one counselor and a few meetings. Sometimes outside professionals must be contacted. As in the drug-counseling program, someone is always there to help.

Youths make use of the program. We have had some suicide threats, but no suicides.

We have another group of students who suffer from jumbled priorities, traumatic experiences, misplaced affections, and other problems that prevent them from getting focused or started and lead to a lack of self-esteem.

I studied various programs at work in schools in different parts of the nation, and put together one of our own for these sorts of youngsters, a program we call PASS. It is, in part, a sort of group therapy session, one with an open, talkative format. But another part is more pedagogical in form.

The two teachers I chose to operate the program had special training and obvious skills in understanding human dynamics. They understood how hung up and hurt young people can get from oppressive and confused relationships, as well as from their own misconceptions and fantasies. They started from scratch and had the kids ask and try to answer the question, "Who am I?" Using a wide array of symbols (the beehive, the waves of the sea, the rays of the sun, the Milky Way), they taught the interrelationship of the individual and the group. Thus they taught justice and equity, as they went along to decision-making, priority setting, and self-esteem.

The PASS program is a necessity, considering the variously downtrodden freshmen we receive each year. And it's a huge success. Kids really do perk up when they realize that other people, grown-ups especially, care. They wake up to the opportunity of an education. They begin to plan their futures. They get a little Eastside spirit.

PASS and most of the other Eastside programs are not instituted or funded by the district, the state, or any government organization. Eastside raises funds where it can. The program teachers are dedicated volunteers. That's why the programs are so alive and successful. None is a bureaucratic hideout. We don't shirk responsibility.

One of our teachers started a choir. Independent from the curricular glee clubs, the choir is for anyone who wants to sing. It meets before or after school, and has become a marvelous success. Kids love to sing. Furthermore, kids are too full of noisy, vacuous, meretricious tripe from the radio. They get caught up in vain imitations, cults of personality, and the mere pretence of song. They need to really sing, to learn to sing from the heart. The choir fills that need.

Inspired by this first extracurricular choir, one of our Hispanic teachers organized a similar choir for students who want to sing in Spanish. Another success. Each choir produces some truly beautiful music. Each has put on well-received performances at student assemblies.

Music is a wonderful companion to spirit. Not only do we have a unique rendition of the alma mater each morning, but a steady stream of various types of music is piped through the halls throughout the day: it is played low enough to cause no distractions, yet it tempers the rigors of our discipline and provides an at-home atmosphere, giving the students just that measure of relaxation that allows for mental clarity.

Musical assemblies were unthinkable before our reforms, because chaos was just too dominant. But now we have weekly musical performances. Talented individuals from the community, or people from other places who have heard of our efforts, regularly volunteer their time and come to entertain and enrich the knowledge and experience of our students. We have hosted jazz combos, classical ensembles, rock groups, rap groups, bluegrass fiddlers, salsa bands, gospel singers, blues singers, cabaret performers, musical theater performers, and a capella chorales. We have also had a wide variety of dancers, acrobats, comedians, magicians, and mimes who have performed on our auditorium stage for appreciative youths, who have learned that an orderly school is far from being a *stalag*.

These many adults, the majority of them successful blacks and Hispanics, come to Eastside because they realize that here their contributions have the chance to mean something, that they are not merely shouting into the wind or pouring water into a sieve. If more inner-city schools were like Eastside, more individuals who are inner-city success stories would turn to these schools and help. Nevertheless, though their entertainment is uplifting, I do not consider entertainers or athletes to be the best role models for these youths. Kids idolize the Michael Jacksons and the Menudos, the Dwight Goodens and the Whitney Houstons too much. They do not understand—unless someone like me tells them again and again—how many more broken lives there are than success stories in sports and entertainment. I do not want to reinforce the virulent and bigoted myth that the only way out of the ghetto is a sexy voice or a good right cross. That is why entertainers may entertain on Eastside's stage, but the ones I authorize to speak to the students are people whose expertise and triumphs are in more accessible realms.

Business people have described, at assemblies, their personal struggles and adventures, to give our students vivid images of what it took to succeed in parts of the real world that many inner-city youths, not without sour grapes resentment and racial hatred, regard as closed to them. But look, here in front of us is someone from the same background who is living proof that it can be done. Furthermore, there is Joe Clark saying that we kids have, in the classrooms of Eastside, the means to do it. These appearances stir the spirit in many a young heart.

We have had:

- Wally (Famous) Amos, of cookie fame, who pursued his dream of having his own business.
- An artist who carved out a successful career for himself by illustrating medical textbooks.
- The female executive of a public relations firm who told how she had confronted prejudice against her race and her sex and had, through competence and persistence, surmounted these obstacles to become the boss of some of the very individuals who had tried to keep her down.
- A lawyer who told how he twice failed his final examination, but would not give up, studied harder, passed, and now has more clients than he can handle.

We have had dozens of inspiring speakers. They have been a real help. But, frankly, we need more. Every chance I get I send out this cry for help for my students: Give us the Michael Jacksons of science, the Dwight Goodens of history, the Whitney Houstons of mathematics. Send them now because there is no time to lose.

I consider the principal the key figure in awakening and augmenting school spirit. A competent principal will rouse the spirit from the ashes of a decadent school, just as an incompetent principal can mortally wound a thriving school spirit within a year. I have fed Eastside's soul from my own. I gave it numerous transfusions of indefatigable spirit, and revived it.

Every challenge that Principal Joe Clark has successfully met has pumped additional life into Eastside High, additional vigor and hope into administrators, teachers, parents, the community, and, most importantly, the students. They have watched me, born to extreme poverty in a Newark ghetto, triumph again and again, over thugs, bureaucrats, and the whole Babel of pernicious, outworn opinions. They knew that I was fighting, and winning, for them, and they were inspired thereby to fight, and win, for themselves.

The principal is the key. The principal must be able and attuned. He must be ready to beneficially exploit every opportunity. For example:

During the first few years of my administration I received numerous death threats, over the phone and in the mail. I still get one every once in a while, but in those days they were a regular occurrence. These little cowardly obscenities were the products, doubtless, of the petty drug-dealers and their numbskull associates.

A principal has a choice: to walk constantly in fear of (and be rendered ineffectual by) some vermin, or to go about his business insouciantly, trusting in his God, believing in his destiny. I ignored the threats. The secretaries, from answering the phones, were aware of a good number of them, and so, through the grapevine, were many of the adults in the school, and a number of the students. Some people worried that one of the threats might someday be real.

One morning I had just stepped into the main office after my usual rounds, when I was greeted by the worried eyes of the secretary. "What is it, Mrs. Warner?"

She was standing at her desk, telephone in one hand and the other clapped on the transmitter. She had obviously just received a threat and now, not wanting to blurt it out, did not know how to answer me. So she stood there nonplussed, worry all over her face.

Annoyed, I pushed through the small gate and covered the space in a few quick strides. "Give me the phone, Mrs. Warner," I said as I advanced. "Who's on the line, another lunatic?"

She nodded in the affirmative as she handed me the phone. "Hello. This is Joe Clark speaking."

"This is the Cosmic Avenger," rasped a deliberately froggy

voice. "I'm going to blow you and your high school away."

"Get a job," I said. "Then use your first paycheck to see a psychoanalyst."

"Very funny, Mr. Bullhorn," the Cosmic Avenger replied, "but your bullshit is over, because I have sent you a present: a nice little explosive device, powerful enough to blow the whole front off your building, and leave the place dripping with guts and severed limbs."

"Guts?" I said. "What would you know about guts, punk?"

"Keep joking, hotshot, keep joking. But the clock is ticking. You've got less than 20 minutes. Don't believe me? Just look out your window. The bomb's in a green gymbag that's just sitting in the parking lot, real close to the front door. Tick, tick, tick. Bye-bye, tough guy."

I hung up. "Another miscreant," I muttered. "Thinks I'm going to empty out the school so he and his doped-up friends can watch from a porch or parked car. No way."

I went into the adjacent office to have a look out at the parking lot. Mrs. Warner and another secretary were already at the window. "It's there, Mr. Clark," Mrs. Warner squeaked, trying to hold her excited voice to a whisper. "The bomb is out there!"

I scowled at her indiscretion. The other secretary, who had followed Mrs. Warner simply because she had looked so apprehensive, gasped. "That's what's in the gymbag? A bomb? Oh my God!"

"Hold on a moment, Mrs. Craig," I said. "We don't know what, if anything, is in the gymbag."

No sooner were my words out, however, than I distinctly heard "bomb!" anxiously whispered in the office behind me. Someone else had been standing near the door, wondering what all the veiled excitement was about. I considered darting back into the other room and demanding that no one breathe another syllable about the alleged bomb. But in the next instant I realized that that would cause fear to increase by the second. So I simply shot Mrs. Warner a reproachful glare and stepped to the window.

There on the tarmac, near the curb slightly to the right of the front steps, sat the green gymbag. I glanced at my watch. Four minutes until the period ended and the corridors filled with kids. Four minutes until word of the suspect gymbag spread rapidly. So be it. I returned to my office and got the head of security on the walkie-talkie.

"Mr. Cooper, I have three important orders for you," I said, "to be carried out at once. First, contact the gatehouse guard. Tell him to close the gate and permit no one on the premises until further notice. Second, tell all door guards to allow no one, under any circumstances, to leave the building until further notice. And third, don't you or any guard go near that green gymbag that's sitting outside the front door." I paused a moment. "Because, Mr. Cooper, I've been told there's a bomb inside it."

"A bomb!"

"Yes, Mr. Cooper, a bomb."

"But Mr. Clark, Mr. Clark, shouldn't we be calling the Fire Department, and the police, and the bomb squad, and, and evacuating every . . . !"

"Mr. Cooper, have you suddenly been promoted to principal?" Finally he muttered, "No, Mr. Clark, no I have not."

"Then you are still head of security."

"Yes, sir, yes I am."

"Then please enact the three orders I have just given you— quickly, Mr. Cooper—and let me handle the gymbag."

"Yes, sir."

Just as I finished with him there was a knock on the door. "Come in."

While the door was swinging open, I could plainly hear several excited voices in the outer office. Enter Mrs. Judkins, one of the vice principals. "Mr. Clark, it's about the. . . ."

"Bomb in the gymbag. Of course."

"You don't think it could be the real thing?" she said. The growing apprehensiveness had gripped her and given her voice a higher pitch. "It only takes one, Mr. Clark, only one that isn't bogus. We know the drug dealers hate you. Do you think it wise to risk the lives of all these children, because you don't. . . ."

"Mrs. Judkins, would you please get control of yourself." I stood up. "No one is going to get the least bit injured." The period bell sounded. "Come with me."

All eyes were on me as I entered the outer office and stepped to the P.A. The word, I thought, is certainly out by now. "Attention everyone!" I announced. "There will be no change in the regular schedule. Everyone, students and teachers alike, will proceed at once to your next regularly scheduled class. I repeat, no change in the schedule." I turned, met the anxious eyes and worried faces, went back into my office, and shut the door.

Now everyone was anxious. I could feel the nervousness of 3,500 human beings pulsating through the floors and walls to center on myself and that green gymbag. Exactly what I wished. "Mr. Cosmic Avenger," I said softly, as I lifted the Louisville slugger from its stand, "you have indeed sent me a present, the opportunity to bid a dramatic and wonderfully symbolic good riddance to drug dealing scum like yourself."

I knew there was no bomb in the gymbag. The punks I was dealing with had neither the means to procure powerful explosives nor the know-how to make a bomb. They were not the Medelin cartel or another enormous drug-trafficking organization. Granted, some grand exalted slimy leader of such an organization could, conceivably, have hired some punk to kill me (and scores of other innocent people) and could have provided the creature with the device. But that notion, which a few of my subordinates had suggested, had no basis in reality, because Joe Clark has not, unfortunately, crippled, or even seriously hurt, the overall black market drug business of northern New Jersey. Drug use at the high school had ceased, utterly. Drug use among youths in the surrounding neighborhoods (based upon the number of cases handled by the juveniles unit of the Paterson police) was down by approximately 40 percent since our Eastside revolution. But drug use in the region, in the state, and in the nation, was steadily increasing. The drop in the street price of cocaine is proof of that.

No drug lord, I thought, is going to risk murder charges simply to bump off someone who is no threat (no short-range threat, at any rate) to his profits. When principals throughout the country take my advice and run drugs out of their schools, then perhaps some gangster will put a contract out on me. In that case, I would consider it an honor. But this threat was from mere punks, howling in their impotence. If I were to give in and empty the school, it would show everyone that the drug punks still had some power over Eastside, and could even frighten Joe Clark. Rather, I would use this "present" to deliver the drug dealers a spiritual *coup de grace*.

Yet, for one moment, a doubt loomed: what if there really was a bomb? To hell with that. What I stood to gain was well worth the risk.

Armed with the baseball bat I stepped out of my office and met the same group of worried faces. "Anybody want the bomb squad?" I said. "Well, you're looking at him."

I walked out and marched swiftly along the corridor. A couple members of my staff were following some paces behind. The hall monitor looked particularly nervous. "You really should quit those cigarettes, Mr. Carlson," I said. "They could kill you."

I came down the inside steps to the main entrance. The guard was standing just inside the door, staring out the window at the object of the moment. He turned at my approach. He was doing his best not to appear frightened. "Morning, Mr. Clark."

"Good morning, Mr. Smith." I brushed by him, pushed open the door. I went down the steps, right for the green gymbag, and stood before it, leaning on the bat. I was facing the school. At the windows of every front classroom were the anxious faces of students and teachers. Staff members watched from the doors. Guards watched from across the parking lot. I had an audience of about 180. "So," I said loudly, for those at the open windows, "this is what a doped-up punk calls a bomb."

I took a stance, swung the bat, and lifted the gymbag 12 feet into the air. One hundred and eighty sets of eyes watched it briefly sail, then drop. It hit the tarmac with a slight, dull sound, skidded several inches, then fell over on one side. "Some bomb!" I declared, and walked over to it.

It was caved in where I had whacked it. I proceeded to pummel it flat with the bathead. Then I picked it up, opened it, and showed the empty gymbag to the audience. "Empty as a drug addict's threat," I said. "And almost as empty as his brain." I tossed it down. "Now let's get on with the business of learning."

That one event did more for school spirit at Eastside than ten undefeated football seasons would ever have done.

In April of 1988 we had a carnival. A fundraiser for extracurricular programs, it proved to be a grand affair, lasting four days (after school on Thursday and Friday, and all day Saturday and Sunday). We rented a ferris wheel and a tilt-a-whirl and four or five other rides. Concessioners set up a wide variety of game-of-chance booths, and people from the Home School Councils and other community residents operated refreshment stands. The fair attracted huge crowds every day and night. The Police Department supplied us with a few officers to direct traffic outside the grounds.

But we did not require any officers to keep the peace or to make any arrests throughout the four-day event. We were set up on the back lawn, facing the street where the Five Percenter fight had broken out three years before. No Five Percenter or racist agitation now. No drugs, no drunkenness, no fights, no thefts, no sexual assaults. No negative incident whatsoever. Just a lot of spirited fun.

People regularly came up to me during the carnival to comment on the great transformation of Eastside High. One man from out of town asked me how Eastside chose the ghost for an emblem.

"Well, sir," I replied, "the school is built on land that was, at one time, a cemetery."

"Oh!" he said, a little surprised.

I smiled. "I like the name for a number of reasons. For one, it suggests a certain fearlessness. Secondly, Eastside itself, over the past six years, has come back from the dead." The old gentleman and the several other people standing with us smiled and nodded their agreement, while barkers cried "Take a chance!" and calliope music played.

"And thirdly," I said to those smiling faces on that peaceful night, "I like the name because a ghost is a spirit, and we've got a lot of that here."

Insight F
SPORTS IN PERSPECTIVE
•

I am not a sports nut, but over the years I have fired quite a few coaches. I fire them for dismal won-lost records. It is nothing personal; often I like the coach I feel obliged to replace. And it's not because I overemphasize athletics, as some principals and schools do. Quite the contrary.

I know that sports have their place—that honest competition, and striving to excel and to win, are characteristics worth inculcating in youths. I also know that these same characteristics can be learned, and to more favorable effect, in the classrooms of a competent and disciplined school motivated by a true, encompassing spirit. Indeed, while the state requires only that a student maintain a passing grade average in order to compete in high school sports, I have raised the standards at Eastside: a C average and a passing mark in each class each marking period, or you are (no exceptions) off the team. This policy puts the proper emphasis on academics, and removes any temptation certain sports-crazy teachers might have to pass some star athlete who doesn't deserve it. It is highly improbable (because of our strict monitoring) that anyone deserving an F will instead receive a D. But if a failing student ever got a C, I would have that derelict teacher's tenured or untenured head. Winning is great, winning is what I and every other Eastsider wants. But education is greater. No coach under my regime will be permitted to recruit failing students to represent this institution of learning, regardless how many games or trophies they might win.

Then why do I fire losing coaches? Because losing is a bad habit. It is particularly bad for an inner-city sports team, because inner-city people are so sick of losing, and inner-city kids are too ready to block out the possibility of winning in any realm. I, as principal, must strive to keep a rightly focused spirit high and lively in every area that pertains to the school. Sports is such an area. We want to show the world that an inner-city school with high academic standards can win on the field as well. And win we eventually will, if it means changing coaches more often than George Steinbrenner does managers.

13

LEADERSHIP AND MANAGEMENT COME HOME

CURRENT MANAGEMENT theory, as taught in colleges of business administration, denotes five major, interrelated facets, or functions, of proper management. These are planning, organizing, staffing, directing, and controlling. Every good manager should perform each of these functions well.

I feel that I have performed all five of those functions well at Eastside High. The old Eastside produced drug addicts and criminals, unwed mothers and welfare cases. Thousands of underdeveloped youths lacking direction and skills were poured out upon the bleak streets of Paterson and upon the nation. The new Eastside turns out responsible, drug-free young citizens ready to work to achieve their goals and make worthy contributions to society. My management accomplished this.

But my managerial method is not strictly by the textbook.

Current theory lists two prerequisites for the successful manager: clearheadedness and the ability to work through people. Absolutely true. Yet I would add another requirement to the list, even put it at the top, because without this attribute the other two cannot carry the day. I am speaking of the instinct for leadership: the desire and the innate drive to be a leader.

The theorists do, under various headings (working through people, directing, controlling), *imply* that this quality is necessary, but it should be emphasized. When your superintendent and your board of education are searching for an individual to serve as your children's principal, leadership must rank high among the searchers' criteria. Especially if it is a troubled school in need of reform.

If leadership is not emphasized in the search and selection, you risk ending up with someone who performs the managerial functions well enough, at least at first, but only within the crippling parameters of the status quo. He or she may well understand the problems, be genial, sympathetic, and able to articulate plans for some necessary reforms, but will he or she have the courage and strength of real leadership to actually get something done?

I think real leaders are born, not made. But I also believe that many potential leaders are unmade: some by the circumstances of their early lives, and others through a systematic indoctrination in timidity.

Regarding the first sort, I assuredly am not in the habit of making excuses for failures. But I also recognize that youths must be guided away from foolishness and evil, and toward more beneficial activities, if we are ever going to snap the cycle of failure. As an educator I am the guide who says to them again and again: "Make the most of difficult and untoward circumstances. When you fall down, get up again. There is no excuse for failure." By such means I steer some away from destruction. But many have had no one to tell them there is no excuse, and have learned instead to hate and blame, and pursue crime, vice, dependency, and despair. And there were those among them with leadership qualities, who might have helped, but now are lost.

I, on the other hand, despite growing up in the Newark ghetto with its numerous hardships, was fortunate. The reason is that I was introduced into the church during my teen years and there learned many lessons from the Bible. Some of these lessons made especially profound impressions upon my young mind. One was the lesson of the Judgment Day: that each individual will be held accountable for his deeds. Another was the meta-phoric advice to build your house on a strong foundation. A third was the parable about the fool who buried his endowment in the ground, while his wiser colleagues invested theirs.

I learned to respect the property of others, knowing that they had worked to obtain it. I realized that if I was going to reject a life of crime and dependency—which became my heartfelt in-tent—then I too must work to fulfill my needs and desires. I looked around and saw that many people were building on very weak foundations: stealing, taking dope, getting drunk, hanging around and acting tough, blaming it all on Whitey. It did not take going to church for me to recognize that I was black, a member of a socially and economically oppressed minority. But I do think religion helped teach me that whining and wasting time were foolish. We were all God's children, white, black, yellow, or anything else, and each of our lives was being viewed in utter fairness. I was meant to work with my endowment—my time and intellect—and make the best of things. Someday I would be judged as to how well I used these gifts. I was determined not to come up short.

Very soon after deciding to eschew crime and vice, and to tread the straight path, it occurred to me that I was going to succeed. I felt through and through that I had made the right choice and that I was not only going to climb out of poverty and want, but was also going to do some good for other people. I was going to somehow inspire them to abandon their foolishness and to build on a strong foundation. I felt this, even though I was just a high school kid working two after-school jobs to help make ends meet at home.

I was seeing the results of my work in my pay, and seeing the results of my studying in my grades. I realized that it was difficult to both work and do well in school, yet I was doing just that. And those facts reinforced my feeling of ultimate success, they confirmed that I was on the right road.

On my own early, disciplining myself, managing my affairs, I built up confidence and character through earnest effort. Though I do not wish my youth's experience on anyone, I do labor incessantly at inculcating self-discipline, self-manage-ment, and self-reliance in all the students who come into my charge. I also think that we, as a nation, should go back to emphasizing these essential virtues in our schools, our homes, and our churches. We can no longer take it for granted that our kids are going to realize the value of these qualities and strive for them.

At Eastside I send unambiguous messages every day. I am an active, visible example and role model of these attributes, and I demand that the teachers be similar role models. At our assemblies, we parade self-reliant individuals and role models in leadership and management before the student body, and through so many of our extracurricular programs we encourage their leadership and management propensities. While we are telling them that their attitudes and decisions will affect their futures, our strict disciplinary regulations unequivocally inform them that their present behavior also bears consequences. In order to avoid my discipline, they discipline themselves, and in time they learn the worth of self-discipline. They really will thank me later. I know because many already have.

There is so much more that can be done throughout the nation in this area, especially if enough people wake up to the need to stop producing, on the one hand, so many pliant milquetoasts and leeches and, on the other, bandits. A renewed emphasis on self-reliance will not only create more responsible citizens all around, but also will certainly assist those youths with leadership potential in stepping forward and receiving the guidance and knowledge they need to properly use their gifts, thus benefiting the whole society. Keep in mind that they are the sort of individuals who, if they do not learn to do good, will do damage.

Before I chose education as a career I seriously considered criminology, because I detested the pilfering of the fruits of another's labor, and hated even more the destruction of innocent lives, especially through senseless violence and the horrid entanglement of drug addiction. Not only had I viewed hellish scenes a-plenty on the streets of my early youth, but, while attending college classes during the day, I worked the night shift as an orderly at a Newark hospital. The victims of crime who regularly staggered or, more often, were carried through the doors—mostly people of my own race and, usually, victimized by other people of my own race—wrenched my heart.

There were also, however, the young girls, pregnant with children doomed to fatherless penury, the people who could neither pay their bills nor fill out the forms, and all the pitiable old people in need of financial assistance. What, I asked myself, could a crime-fighter do for these people? On every floor, in every room of the hospital there was misfortune. There was more sorrow and pain in the houses stretching away from each side of the hospital. Victimized lives, wasted lives, mismanaged lives. I already felt I had some power to exert in this world, and I wanted to exert it to somehow ease the suffering and stop the madness. But how? How to really make a difference?

Walking to class one morning, wrestling with this problem of what career to pursue to make my life a truly meaningful one, I paused to look at the school buildings, and at the students and teachers moving across the modest campus. I gave some deep thought to what education means, especially to poor, minority youths. And it came over me, standing there transfixed like a tree, that a genuine, dedicated educator could probably do more to improve the lot of the innocent than a crime-fighter. The latter, however necessary and however much committed to the task, has a more limited range of lives he can influence, and is usually acting in a last-resort capacity, usually with the harm already done. But an educator works near the roots of a wider range of problems. He has the chance to cancel all sorts of wickedness by steering youths in more wholesome directions and fortifying them for life's struggles with knowledge and skills. An educator can be instrumental in laying the foundations for decent homes, thus starting a sort of benevolent chain-reaction militating against future evils. It would be, I thought, a less glamorous career, but a more effective one. I decided to become a teacher.

By the time I entered graduate school at Seton Hall I had widened the scope of my idea of an educator from that of a teacher to an administrator as well. This was, for me, quite a natural progression. I was meant to be a leader, I just knew it. A teacher influences a few classes, an administrator influences a whole school, or a whole school system. I aimed high, like Thoreau suggested, and earned my masters in administration. Though I started off in the Paterson system as a grade school teacher, I never abandoned my higher goal.

I realize that it is a cynical age, and that there is a conventional mind-set which says that people only act out of self-interest. In a way, I suppose, that is true for me as well, but in no mean fashion. It is in my own interest to do great and influential things. I would not be satisfied if I did not have worthy challenges to take on and people to benefit. It has always made me feel good inside to know for a fact that I have helped a youth toward a richer life. It gives my self joy, and even hope, to think that I have assisted people to make this a better world. My self is quite interested in further joy and further hope. *My self is interested in pulling the education system out of hell and decay.*

I did not choose the teaching profession because it was an easy one, or the only one available. I certainly did not choose it for the money. I might have made more on the detective squad, or driving a truck, or managing a store. I chose education because my self was interested in helping others, especially youths. I believe everybody should be interested in that.

My decision to choose education over criminology indicates a preference of the method of prevention-management over crisis-management, though I was unaware of those terms at the time.

During my college years, reading the histories and the newspapers, and observing the actions of teachers, merchants, students, and working people, it became increasingly apparent to me that the Divine system of accountability for deeds was also a perfect model for how affairs should proceed in the day-to-day world. The more I thought about it, the more sense it made. Each job has a description, each position has certain duties: people who do not fulfill the description or meet the duties should be relieved of the job. Upon diligent study, I recognized that the civilized system of the United States, for all its flaws and inequities, strives in its basic forms of government and enterprise to adhere to this concept of accountability, and that the inequities within the system can best be corrected by efforts within the system.

At the time of the Civil Rights Movement, the black leaders were, peacefully and within our civilized system, demanding that the governments of the Southern states be held accountable for ignoring the law of the land, specifically the Fourteenth Amendment. In Alabama in 1964, Martin Luther King, Jr., and his colleagues planned a huge protest march from Selma to Montgomery, the state capital. The State of Alabama refused to issue a permit for the march, thus dubbing it illegal. That meant that the police would take action, assuredly violent action, against marchers. Despite a great deal of protest from many of his allies, King postponed the march until his organization could obtain a federal court order allowing the protestors to proceed.

The more radical blacks were willing to force a bloody confrontation, which would gain them martyrs, sympathy and support, and maybe even a revolution. But King held the most power and he decided, for the safety of the marchers and the good name of the whole movement, that they would work within the system. In a week's time, through the efforts of President Johnson, the court order was issued. The march proceeded, under federal protection, without violence or illegality.

The Southern states were held accountable. A great deal of segregation was abolished. The chief gain of the Civil Rights Movement is that the concept of equal opportunity became reality: that all citizens have accessibility to the competition, in equity and within the law, for material needs and desires. This concept was made real through leadership working within the system. Among the radicals who split with King shortly after the Montgomery march were several individuals with excellent leadership potential, which was, unfortunately, led astray by rage, vengeance, hate, and vanity. Their legacy, developed in cahoots with conniving liberal politicians, includes the degrading quota system, the debilitating welfare system, the dumbed down academic requirements for minorities, and the overall increase in crime, drugs, and the leech mentality of the inner cities.

I had decided on being a leader for change within the system before Johnson (or Kennedy) was president. I was against the quota system years before they had a name for it. While Martin Luther King, Jr., was in Alabama, I was in Paterson, organizing black and Hispanic teachers to demand, peacefully and within the law, that the Paterson educational system be held accountable for blocking minority educators out of certain deserved jobs, administrative posts in particular. Some minority candidates were obviously better qualified than some whites who had gotten the jobs. I—relatively new to the school system, but confident in my abilities—was affronted by the blatant injustice. I put our group together. We made demands to the board for equity in appointments. We started to get encouraging results.

I had a lot of good ideas concerning accountability, competence, and discipline, much like my ideas today, though perhaps
a little less sophisticated. But people tend to see an image more
than listen to a message, especially when image and message are
coming from an unknown quantity, as I was to Paterson in those
days. I liked to wear dashikis then, and I felt a genuine pride in
the awakening of my people to their cultural roots. But politically I was very much as I am now, basically a conservative, all
for free enterprise and protecting the tenets of the Constitution.
But the Paterson school authorities of that time did not bother to
study the many things I was saying. They saw only a young black
man in a dashiki leading a movement for reform along racial
lines. This was the era of riots in Watts, Detroit, and Newark.
The board reacted to our agitation in a diplomatic and frightened
manner. They appointed some minority candidates simply because they were black and Hispanic. Never mind that what I had
proposed from the outset was promotion according to the sole
criterion of the best qualified, regardless of race. We were
strapped with a quota system that would invalidate and under-
mine our movement.

I protested. These individuals are not qualified, I said, and
should not have been appointed. The organization I had started,
however, would not heed me. What was wrong with me, they
complained. Why was I bent on ruining the great victory? The
board, flaunting its liberalism, also chose not to understand my
simple message. I suppose they reckoned that I, too, was motivated by the lust for political power. Suddenly, from front and
back I was pegged as little more than a troublemaker. My former
allies turned their ethical tails and slipped away. The board
realized I was isolated, so they shipped me across town, to a
grammar school in an all-white neighborhood, where I would
have no one to organize and nothing to complain about. For ten
years, like Ulysses, I was exiled.

It was a setback for the leader in me, but, in the long run, it
proved a blessing in disguise. I had learned a valuable lesson
about human nature: Never trust anyone. I do not mean this in a
moral sense alone, as if to say that all humans are scoundrels.
Most humans are not. But many humans who are not scoundrels
are often tempted, cajoled, or intimidated into actions that are
unwise or unethical. It is a universal human proclivity to move

along the line of least resistance, which often amounts to "taking the easy way out," regardless that the harder way is the proper one. If people cannot be clearly shown that it is to their advantage to do the more difficult thing, they will not, unless they are coerced. When the student in a management class is informed that he must learn to work through other people, he is not necessarily taught the lesson I learned.

I also acquired a great deal of first-hand knowledge of kids in those years. Kids desire discipline, because order is necessary for learning to take place, and everyone has an inborn desire to learn and be prepared for life. At the same time, kids resent mere regimentation, because it tends to belittle their vibrant individuality. They love adults who recognize these things, and who are honest with them. They want adults they can look up to. I respected the kids as human beings and individuals, while infusing my every class with the enthusiasm I felt for bettering mankind through education, and the youngsters responded. It was invigorating. It was fun. Though I resented what the educational bureaucracy had done to me, I came to believe that I indeed had chosen the right career.

I never abandoned my dream of one day becoming an administrator. In order to try my hand at management, I applied for and obtained a job with Essex County (bordering Passaic County, in which Paterson is located) as the director of camps and playgrounds. (My straight A's in administration at Seton Hall spoke loudly in my support.) The bulk of my duties took place in the summer, but the work was lively all year round. Combined with my teaching duties, I was kept plenty busy. Indeed, the stamina I had exerted in my teen years, studying and working, not only did not desert me, but increased under the added pressure of being responsible for 15,000 to 20,000 youths. That I was beginning to do what I truly love to do—to manage—has to be the major factor for my indefatigability.

In my active years in this obscure directorship I was able to combine my concept of across-the-board accountability with that basic, healthy distrust I had gained for human behavior, to form the complete and precise managerial method that has since become my hallmark.

I learned to think of the long-range ramifications of actions. I also became increasingly aware of how the powers-that-be would react. This intuitive knowledge definitely did not intimidate me. It did, however, make me wise enough to walk away from battles I could not win, as well as to be prepared beforehand for the inevitable counterattacks when I did deem it worth the risk to cross swords with higher-ups.

I learned, too, that no matter how highly positioned a manager is, he or she must be well-acquainted with the details of the duties of all subordinates from the lowest to the highest, so that the manager/supervisor is able to understand the entire operation, to organize effective monitoring for all performances, to readily find the cause of any trouble, to move swiftly and deftly to correct any error, and to build true *esprit de corps*.

I clearly defined the hierarchy and the duties of each rank. To tighten and strengthen my system, I adapted and expanded the process of written requests and reports, so that there were exact, informative, and readily available paper trails up and down the chain of command.

And I was there in person, every day, the epitome of the hands-on manager, to set the example for commitment and the tempo of operations, and to keep the focus properly on the well-being of the children.

By these means I kept a constant eye on all facets of my responsibility. Competence was the scale on which each underling was weighed. If you did not efficiently do your job, I invariably and swiftly found out and you, swiftly and invariably, were gone. My directorship won well-deserved praise. More importantly, I confirmed my managerial ability to myself. My innate desire for leadership had not languished in exile: it was livelier than ever. I was more than ready for an administrative position in Paterson. At a time when there were a number of schools without real principals, I was a real principal without a school.

My opportunity came in the late 1970s, when I was offered a job no one else wanted: principal of PS 6, the worst-behaved grammar school in the city, with an atrocious academic rating. I eagerly accepted. I knew I could turn that school around. I recall even tracking down one parent, who had withdrawn her children from PS 6 in fear and disgust just a few days before my appointment, and beseeching her to return them.

"Madame, now is not the time to give up on School 6," I said, standing on her run down porch. "I am the new principal. I am the one who can give your children the education they deserve. If I did not care, would I be standing here? I have the ability. I have the will. Please, give me the chance!"

She did. And soon became one of my staunchest supporters. Most of the parents of children at PS 6 (which is in the same depressed part of town as Eastside High) eventually became Joe Clark's supporters and allies. I applied my method, energy, and love, and brought about exemplary order and head-turning academic improvement. PS 6 became known, first to parents, then the local newspapers, and finally the ruling educational bureaucracy, as "The Miracle on Carroll Street." It was because of my work on Carroll Street that Superintendent Napier offered me that other job no one else wanted, at Eastside.

And it was because of my success at Carroll Street that, once I decided to consider the Eastside post, I was able to demand the complete support, financial and political, which I required to get the job done. At last I was beginning to exert the sort of power a real leader should be able to, and here, finally, was a task and challenge worthy of my skills.

Immediately upon accepting the position as Eastside's principal, I gathered up the old and deplorably inadequate manuals, regulations, and instruction sheets for the high school, and sat down at my desk to write new ones. These make up the school's constitution. I am the school's benevolent dictator. I wrote the manuals that first year, and have written and updated them every year since. The only item I will delegate is the compilation of some lists, which I thoroughly check. I am aware of every syllable of this constitution. I make certain it is crystal clear and inclusive right down to details.

I address my administrators:

"Each individual is uniquely endowed with certain talents and deficiencies. It is obvious that we cannot perform in like manners. As administrators, however, there are certain traits that should be clearly manifested. If they are not, it simply means that you are certainly incapable of performing in an acceptable manner.

"The following are a few of the administrative 'musts':

1. You must be knowledgeable in all areas of responsibilities.
2. Support of all school policies must be categorically and diligently enforced.
    a. All changes or alterations in schedules must be submitted to Mr. Jones, the scheduler, for approval by Mr. Clark.
    b. Authority to forward any and all information that is requested may only be given by the principal.
    c. Only the principal and his designee are permitted to use the intercom. It will be used for morning announcements and absolute emergencies, to be determined by the principal or his designee.
3. Loyalty to the principal must be clearly manifested. If you cannot support the principal, it is only fitting and proper that you leave or request a transfer, before you suffer irreparable professional injury.
4. Visibility in corridors and classrooms must be an incessant endeavor.
5. Involvement in extracurricular student and adult functions must be a reality. Failure to participate in the aforementioned negates your effectiveness.
6. Elevating the image of Eastside High School must be an untiring endeavor. Your enthusiasm about our school should be clearly seen by the whole staff. Teachers, in turn, will emulate your behavior.
7. Firmness and fairness must permeate every facet of your being. You cannot afford to accept nonsense from teachers. Attempting to cajole or coax teachers into doing a job they are paid to perform is ludicrous.
8. The ability to make administrative decisions, right or wrong, should be clearly evident.
9. Meeting time lines must be clearly evident.
10. A propensity towards innovation in educational procedures must be ever present."

I see to it that all administrative duties, areas of responsibility, and proper procedures are unmistakably listed. Included in each administrator's handbook are samples of all the various forms (my necessary paper trail) that must be filled out for each designated procedure. The administrative areas and the person or persons in charge of each appear in a complete list alphabetically arranged. For example:

College Visits - Maus/Lyde
Conferences - Maus/Lopas
Curricula - Gamble
Custodians - Mr. Clark
Drug Coordinator - Lyde
Early Teacher Dismissal - Maus
English Department - Gamble/DiMartino

There are about 120 headings, covering everything from scholarships to fire drills. You will note that my name is the only one appearing with a title (Mr.). This holds true throughout the list and is assuredly no accident. The point must be made that one individual is the chief of the entire operation, and that all others are subordinates: one chief, one operation, one purpose.

Of the 11 departments at Eastside, each of the vice principals handles the administration of two or three, while each department has a chairperson or head chosen by the Board of Education—in the English Department, Mrs. Gamble is the vice principal, Mrs. DiMartino the department head. The building itself is divided by floors into four districts (Basement to 3rd Floor), each the responsibility of one of the vice principals, each of whom has a number of assistants appointed from the department heads and the teaching corps. This entire breakdown appears on a separate page, with the notation that each respective administrator "will be responsible for repair and maintenance requests in his or her area. This includes rooms, offices, halls and stairwells."

Ever since the first several weeks of the 1982 school year, the word has been out at Eastside that Joe Clark enforces his regulations. It should go without saying that encyclopedias filled with regulations are just piles of paper if there is not enforcement. When I write that the administrator in charge of this or that floor is responsible for repair requests, that administrator knows that I (during my 22 miles a day) will undoubtedly notice any disrepair or maintenance needs. If a request form has not been filed, I will want to know why. If one has and nothing further has been done, I will take it to the chief custodian. My administrators know that when they cease making administrative decisions I will consider them to have abdicated their positions. I will make certain they abdicate in fact as well.

Each vice-principal is in charge of a year of students, so that requests for various freshman concerns must go through Mrs. Maus, sophomore through Mr. Tyson, and so on. There is a separate page stating the office number and telephone extension of all administrative personnel.

In problem schools, especially in the inner city, cafeterias are halls of chaos. No longer at Eastside. My instructions to the teachers and administrators who monitor the cafeteria clearly reflect my desire to keep things that way.

For example:

"2. Be alert for situations that have the potential of flaring up into physical conflict. Step in before it starts."

(I include that advice every year, though there has not been a fight in the Eastside cafeteria throughout the six years of my watch. But monitors have acted to defuse possible fights. That advice is part of the reason for the peace, and I will go on including it.)

"3. Constantly remind students of their responsibilities and expected conduct. Stress neatness and cleanliness."
"6. Teachers on cafeteria supervision duty are not permitted to sit down or congregate with other teachers."
"8. Be on time."
"10. Students should not be permitted to roam about the cafeteria. They can be in their seats, outside, or in the activities room."

The students, of course, are aware (or damn well ought to be) of the cafeteria regulations and the penalties for infractions. The list of rules and penalties (which is set down in Chapter 2) appears in each student manual, also in the administrators' manual, and is posted in prominent places throughout the building, and distributed to every teacher.

The administrators' manual, in addition, contains my guidelines for handling infractions, and the information is also presented to each teacher. Under the heading of Major Infractions I list fighting, assault, smoking, drug use, and any activity that threatens the life, safety, or health of the violator or someone else. In such cases the violator is to be sent at once to the teacher-assistant in charge of discipline. Most of our problems, when we have any, fall into the category of Minor Infractions. That does not mean we take these matters lightly. On the contrary, if the teacher has not been able to settle the problem by conferring with the student and, if necessary, with the student's parent, then there is a complete step-by-step referral system outlined, from the teacher to the department head to the teacher-assistant and myself, with each adult in the chain filling out and forwarding a form stating what is happening, why, when, and to whom.

There is a correct procedure for suspension, for re-admittance following suspension, and for academic assignments during suspension. Procedures exist as well for monitoring tardiness and for collecting attendance lists. All are set down in the manual and each procedure has, of course, its forms for the administrators and teachers to sign, so that there is always an up-to-date record, including who was responsible for what. When a teacher, for example, does not have an attendance card ready for the administrator's delegate, or it is discovered that the attendance has been erroneously taken, that teacher will receive a notice from me, informing the teacher that the slip-up will be included in his or her evaluation.

The meticulous evaluation of teachers is the responsibility of the different department heads, who must file written reports with their respective vice principals on specified dates. Tenured teachers receive one formal evaluation per school year, nontenured teachers receive three. But I impress upon the administrators that the evaluation process is an ongoing thing, and suggest that they stay as attentive to their teachers as I do to both teachers and administrators. I also write the guidelines for the department heads, urging them to be mindful of more than 40 evaluative criteria. That list includes:

for the classroom:
- The teacher's initiation, development, and ending of the lesson
- The summary and the introduction of the next day's lesson, and the homework assignment
- The teacher's poise, voice control, grammar, grooming
- The physical arrangement of the classroom, and the seating arrangement

- The general classroom appearance: is it cheerful, warm, inviting? Is there evidence of the students' work displayed?
- Student attentiveness
- How was the chalkboard used?
- The teaching method: lecture? demonstration? did the pupils participate in experiments? in self-discovery?
- Were the teacher's questions well-phrased? did they provoke thought?
- How was the teacher's behavior toward students: respectful? rigid? informal? nervous?

for other duties:

- Accuracy of attendance records
- Study hall organization
- Corridor supervision
- Punctuality
- Supervision of fire drills

I remind the evaluators to address both the teacher's strengths and weaknesses, and to hold conferences with the teachers concerning their assessments. There are few teachers, I say, so excellent as to need no improvement in certain areas.

And there is an extensive list of the other responsibilities of department heads, including hall monitoring, holding regular department meetings, providing substitute teachers with all they require, making sure that all teachers submit weekly lesson plans, supervising discipline, and requisitioning needed materials.

Requisitioning has a step-by-step procedure to ensure proper approval (by me) and complete fairness in the handling of checks and vouchers. This applies to all departments and personnel, from vice principals and guidance directors to janitors and secretaries. I have an eye on all materials and funded activities: cans of paint and bus trips, boxes of staples and microscope slides. The depositing of money into the school treasury (where all activities' money must go without exception) also has a precise formula, painstakingly designed to prevent any errors or other misfortunes.

Yes, other schools and organizations have such regulations and procedures. The difference is that we have no dead letters at Eastside. All our rules are vital. We need them to keep the operation tight, to optimally serve our overall purpose. Paperwork does not usually appeal to me—I would rather be roaming the halls, kibitzing with the students. But writing and correcting the manuals never bores me, because I know their value and their power, because I can feel the instructions in beneficent motion even as the pen touches the paper.

The Guidance Department too has its list of responsibilities: counseling, dissemination of guidance information, liaisons with outside agencies, surveys and follow-up studies, enrollments for summer school, scholarships, maintaining students' cumulative folders, and so forth. Counselors are assigned to offices, their available hours are posted, and their telephone extensions are listed in the administrators' manual.

The teachers, in their booklet, are informed of their supervisory duties, such as posting themselves in the middle of the corridor between classes, monitoring the corridors when assigned, and conducting study halls that are conducive to study. Along with the reminder to submit weekly plan books to their department heads, the nontenured teachers are provided with a lesson plan format that they are required to follow:

"1. Goal—general statement of long-range purpose
  2. Objectives—yours as a teacher, and the performance you expect from the students
  3. Materials
  4. Procedure—chronological order of activities
  5. Method
  6. Homework

"Lesson plans will be monitored carefully and reviewed by the department chairperson and the delegated administrator during each observation." Of course, a faulty lesson plan will be noted in a teacher evaluation.

Some people think it unnecessary to monitor teachers for logical thought in planning. That's a naive view.

Teachers are reminded to keep their classrooms clean, and locked when not in use, and to maintain neat and concise seating charts and roll books. We want our teachers to do their jobs, and we feel they should, as professionals, be able to take the pressure

202 · *Joe Clark with Joe Picard*

of close observation. We also want them, in the extended and full role of teacher, to set worthy examples for the youths we are seeking to rescue from the abyss.

Quite a lot of items are covered in all three manuals: ID regulations, homework policy, transfers, participation in the various clubs, and so on. All of my experience, expertise, and resolve has energetically gone, and still goes, to seeing that everything is covered. In their manual the students are informed of the academic requirements for graduation. They are provided with a complete curriculum description and all the rules and procedures, from required hall behavior to Honor Roll criteria, from listings of their rights and responsibilities to a list of the extracurricular clubs they can join.

On Page 2 of the 1988 student manual, I write:

"We believe that although each student is different, all of our students have academic, vocational, physical and social potential for success in life.

"We believe in nurturing attitudes, values and skills that will provide for and encourage participation in the political, economic, technological, social and cultural processes of this country."

Then I list some of the things our high school, once a snakepit of disorder, crime, and despair, is now effectively concerned with. For example:

- Developing a sense of pride in academic achievement
- Encouraging parental and community involvement in the educational process
- Increasing the self-esteem of each individual student
- Preparing students to compete successfully
- Maintaining a strong administrative structure in order to implement the school's policy of academic excellence
- Maintaining a safe and orderly environment, one conducive to learning

All of the above could just as easily make up a list of reasons why I take the time to write the manuals. And why I am at the building six, sometimes seven, days a week, 10 to 12 hours a day.

I do not say that we at Eastside have as yet reached all our goals. But I do know, and the hard evidence bears me out, that through my leadership and managerial method Eastside has been turned around.

There are people who like to call my managerial method tyrannical. They are usually people who do not have to deal with running a huge inner-city high school (the second largest in New Jersey) on a day-to-day basis, and often people unacquainted with the 1980s ghetto. I am tired of speaking to these people. So I will let a friend of mine, Frank Corrado, formerly one of my vice principals at Eastside, say a little about my "tyrannical" administration.

"Joe Clark understands the value, and the real necessity, of a principal being the sole person in charge, and constantly promotes that. He knows better than most that, in the changeable and potentially explosive atmosphere of an inner-city high school, authority must not be demeaned, or all order may break down. So he monitors himself, as thoroughly as he monitors anyone else, to make certain that he always behaves as a chief administrator should.

"I learned, when I disagreed with Mr. Clark, to wait until we were alone, behind closed doors, to voice my disagreement. In those situations the atmosphere was warm and friendly, and he was quite willing to listen to other opinions, and to take advice. But once he again stepped out before his subordinates, back out into his official capacity of principal, if he declared that four was five, and you were foolish enough to correct him, you would receive a full blast of his wrath. Some people never understood this, and mistook his belief in this style of leadership for a show of arrogance.

"He took me aside once, early in our first year at Eastside, and said, 'To be an effective principal in an inner-city school one must be controversial.' He did not mean that he planned to provoke controversy per se. He meant that erroneous thought and processes had become so endemic to the system that any principal properly doing the job would inevitably meet resistance. Joe Clark always had the courage to do his job properly.

"He taught me to be an effective administrator. He heaped so many responsibilities upon me that I had to learn to juggle duties, prioritize, and realize working potential I did not know I had. . . . He demanded that his administrators make decisions and, right or wrong, be responsible for them. He would not tolerate a wishy-washy sort of person and, in administration, no one should. Most of all, I learned from Joe Clark never to lose sight of the purpose of a career in education, never to lose sight of the kids. He is a kids' principal. He works for them, he listens to them, he loves them. And they love him."

Corrado is presently principal of William R. Satz Intermediate School in Holmdel, New Jersey. Several other people who served under me as administrators have gone on to higher posts in other schools: Glenn Lagatol is presently principal of PS 2 in Paterson; Willi Davis was for several years the successful principal at PS 6, and has been succeeded there by Charles Lighty, also a former vice principal of mine; at PS 3 Audrey Favors is now principal; William Butler presides over PS 13; across town at Paterson's other high school, John F. Kennedy, Bill Toole, who served under me, is presently the lauded principal; and John Rizzo has been named the principal for the Alternate School, the institution that my efforts brought into existence.

It is no coincidence that eight future principals served under me in my six years at Eastside High. The superintendent, readily, and the Board of Education, somewhat begrudgingly, will acknowledge that my administration is used as a training ground for the prospective chief administrators in the Paterson system. There are also about a dozen other of my former assistants serving elsewhere in some level of administrative work, and scores of teachers who have at one time or another come under my influence. This is not to say that any of these people are carbon copies of Joe Clark. Each has his or her own style, which is as it should be. But each has learned some things from me. And each has had the chance to see commitment to the education of youth in action. They now can never honestly say, or self-indulgently think, that real commitment does not exist. They now will be forced to try to be as effective as I am (or even more effective).

The events of my life, especially of the last several years, have turned in a wonderful sort of way, to afford me the opportunity to do some further good for my people, my country, and the human race.

On the first day of classes, in September of 1983, an Associated Press reporter covering urban school openings in the Northeast got wind of us through a local paper and came to Eastside merely to jot down a few lines and be off again. He was, however, very impressed, and decided to write an entire story about the school and myself. Early the next morning the evening news team at CBS read the AP wire and made arrangements to come out and interview me. I was mentioned on the CBS *Evening News* with Dan Rather that same evening. The next day I got a call from Ted Koppel, whose offer to appear on *Nightline* I, rather astonished by the rapid course of unexpected events and with a school to run, turned down. Then, that same day, I received a call from the President of the United States, who must also watch Dan Rather.

By presidential invitation I traveled to the White House, for the first of several visits, and participated in a conference on education. Then, over the next several months, I appeared in a conference on the *Donahue* show, was highlighted with Eastside in a Presidential booklet on education in America, and began accepting offers to speak to various groups and organizations throughout the country, though I never appeared on school time.

I mention these events to point out that my method, my results, and my self came under closer and closer scrutiny from all angles (right, left, center, and variations) as time went on. Connie Chung of NBC News did a television profile of the Clarkian revolution. A movie producer saw it and began showing up in Eastside's outer office at 6:30 each morning in order capture some of my time. I eventually appeared on *Nightline, Crossfire, A Current Affair,* and numerous other television and radio programs. *The Philadelphia Inquirer* and *The New York Times* wrote extensively about me and the transformation at Eastside, and we appeared in newspapers and magazines across the nation. My life was probed, in search of dirt or weakness. Despite some wincing at my style, they found Joe Clark was clean through and through.

When I used my get-things-done brand of leadership to militate effectively for the Alternate School, pushing for the greater good of the students, my local adversaries, thinking I had finally slipped up, were licking their chops. But I had firm support from the two most important levels of our American political structure: the grass roots support of parents, students, and residents, and the support of the White House. Unfortunately for my enemies, I did not fall.

That victory led to my being on the cover of *Time*. It also caused Warner Brothers to stop looking for a major star and a soundtrack to "carry" their Joe Clark movie. They suddenly saw that the story itself was strong enough to do that. Even Hollywood, for all its tinsel and distortion, came to recognize enough of what my revolution meant, to shift the central focus of *Lean on Me* to what is really important: the kids, and how I help them.

My kids learned through all of this. They saw how the media and motion picture industries work. They learned how each industry strays from reality. They became aware of the adult world of jealousies and deceptions. They also became aware of the adult world of genuine achievement. They saw me manage situation after novel and tough situation. They saw me neither twist nor break under pressure. Minority students, poor youths—I gave them a needed role model, a black man born in poverty, who rose in a good cause and through his own efforts to national prominence. I showed them, and I told them, that the media would surely have exposed me for a knave had I been one. I was not an imitation or a fanciful commercial image of a real man. I was and am—through rightful purpose and years of hard work, through building on a strong foundation—a real man. I pointed the way for them, as an educator should.

That morning, in January of 1988, when Secretary Bennett called to voice his support for me in my struggle with the Board of Education, I became aware of the national media as I had never been before. With the TV crews and print reporters waiting anxiously at my office door, pouncing upon me with their cameras and klieg lights, their microphones and pads, I suddenly realized that they not only were probing me. They were also providing me with a lectern, a bully pulpit, and they were able and willing to do this because there was an audience out there, across America, willing to listen.

Because the problems in education in this country are so grave, and because we all must confront them or live with the dire consequences, many people look to where they might find solutions.

I give you the example of myself. I have shown you what one man, a black man born into abject poverty, can accomplish against the odds. Now it is your turn to act and effect change. Help save our schools, our children, and the future of our civilization.

Yes, there is that much at stake. But together we can make the crucial difference. I have seen how righteous actions transcend ethnicity and economic class. Such actions evoke a deep, rushing river of support, which is nothing less than the flow and spirit of humanity. We are the solution to the present crisis in education. We can, we must, and together we will, triumph.